TRAINS OF THE OLD WEST

TRAINS OF THE OLD WEST

⸎ BRIAN SOLOMON ⸎

MetroBooks

PAGE 2: *One of the first Central Pacific trains to pass over the completed Transcontinental Railroad pauses for its portrait along the Humboldt River in Palisade Canyon, located a few miles west of present-day Carlin, Nevada. The Transcontinental Railroad was rushed to completion in 1869, and as a result the tracks were in poor condition.*

An Imprint of Friedman/Fairfax Publishers

Library of Congress Cataloging-in-Publication Data.

Solomon, Brian.
    Trains of the Old West / Brian Solomon.
        p.   cm.
    Includes bibliographical references and index.
    ISBN 1-56799-478-4 (hc)
    1. Railroads—West (U.S.).   I. Title
TF23.6.S65   1997
385'.0978—dc21   97-13126

Editors: Tony Burgess and Ann Kirby
Art Director: Kevin Ullrich
Designer: Galen Smith
Photography Editor: Amy Talluto
Production Manager: Jeanne Hutter

Color separations by Bright Arts Graphics (S) Pte. Ltd.
Printed and bound in China by Leefung-Asco Printers Ltd.
1 3 5 7 9 10 8 6 4 2

For bulk purchases and special sales, please contact:
Friedman/Fairfax Publishers
Attention: Sales Department
15 West 26th Street
New York, NY 10010
212/685-6610   FAX 212/685-1307

Visit our website:
http://www.metrobooks.com

DEDICATION

To my father, Richard J. Solomon, who sparked my interest in railroads.

ACKNOWLEDGMENTS

No project of this sort is accomplished alone, and I would like to thank the many people who helped with this effort, especially: Tony Burgess of Michael Friedman Publishing Group; John Gruber of Pentrex Publishing; Richard Gruber; Paul Hammond of Pentrex Publishing; Tom Hoover, Jr.; Brian L. Jennison; Clark Johnson, Jr.; Robert W. Jones of Pine Tree Press; Mel Patrick; J. D. Schmid; Mike Shafer of Andover Junction Publications; and Maureen and Richard J. Solomon.

Contents

FIRST AND LAST RIDE ON THE NORTH COAST LIMITED

❧

OPPOSITE: *The Northern Pacific's* North Coast Limited *at St. Paul, Minnesota, in September 1969. Unlike other railroads, many of which permitted their passenger trains to deteriorate, the Northern Pacific always maintained its trains to the highest standards.*

In 1970, less than a year before Amtrak assumed operation of most intercity passenger train service in the United States, my parents and I flew to Seattle to ride one of America's great passenger trains before it vanished into history. I recall this great trip as if it happened yesterday, although I was only four years old at the time. The *North Coast Limited* made an indelible impression on my young mind.

Before boarding the famous train, we spent some time seeing the sights, specifically the monorail and the famous Space Needle, leftovers from the 1962 Seattle World's Fair. My mother feared that I might not be sufficiently engaged by the train ride: a quick trip to a toy store provided me with a watercolor set, brushes, and paper. Soon we were off, riding first class on the Raymond Loewy–styled streamliner.

Aboard the train we had our own private room, a small but clean traveling hotel room. To me the best part of the train was the domed observation car, and it was there that I spent most of my two days on the train. There is no better way to see the West than from a glass-top Budd Vista Dome. Northern Pacific boasted one of the only fleets of Vista Dome Lounges, the only domes with tables between the seats. I found this feature handy as we rolled through "Big Sky Country," and I set up my watercolor set and made primitive attempts at documenting the scenery. Without a doubt, Montana has some of the most spectacular scenery in the country.

During the night, we rolled along the Clark Fork, up and over Evaro Hill, east of the appropriately named Paradise, Montana. At dawn, in the vicinity of Silver Bow canyon, we ran parallel to the rails of Milwaukee Road's ill-fated Pacific extension. In 1970 the line was still active and electrified. Soon we began to overtake one of Milwaukee's slow-moving dead freights, which were notorious for derailments. From the dome in the veiled morning light I caught a glimpse of two brown-and-orange, double-ended, baby-faced "Little Joe" electric locomotives. Named for Joseph Stalin, these powerful locomotives were built by General Electric for the Soviet Union in the early 1950s, but the Cold War prevented their delivery, and they were sent to the remote mountains of Montana and Idaho instead.

East of Butte we rolled up and over the Continental Divide on Homestake Pass. The original Northern Pacific mainline ran far to the north, cresting the divide at Mullen Pass, continuing through the state capital at Helena and along the Missouri River. This route, though bypassed by the *North Coast*, was heavily used by freight trains, the lifeblood of the Northern Pacific. Today, the mainline over Mullen Pass still carries freight, while the route I rode, over Homestake, is dormant.

We crossed another summit on Bozeman Pass, and rode through a long tunnel before dropping down into Livingston. The train paused here for a few minutes and we got out to stretch our legs. The Livingston depot is a classic. Designed by the same firm that created New York City's Grand Central Terminal, it exhibits the same level of ornamentation and architectural finesse that the Manhattan structure is known for. Today the Livingston station is beautifully restored and serves as a museum.

Before we left Livingston, I went up to the head end of the train to look at the big, streamlined, two-tone-green Electro-Motive F7 locomotives that were hauling the train. Three locomotives were needed, providing more than five thousand horsepower to bring the train over the Northern Pacific's rugged mountain grades.

Back aboard the *North Coast*, as we ran along the Yellowstone River, I continued with my painting, mailed a postcard from the train, and enjoyed a meal in the dining car. I cannot recall whether or not I had a famous Northern Pacific potato, but I have since been told that a ride on the legendary train was worth it just to eat one. Eastern Montana is not as scenic as the western section. By Billings, the mountains have retreated to the horizon and the level plain predominates.

My mother grew up in Glendive, a town on the Yellowstone River in far eastern Montana. This remote community owes its relative prosperity to the Northern Pacific, which placed locomotive shops and a small yard there. It is also a division point,

where all trains stop to change crews. The *North Coast* paused there for twenty minutes while the train was serviced. My parents revisited the town, but I was afraid that the train would leave without us. I stayed in the dome, viewing downtown Glendive from that safe vantage point.

Early the next morning we arrived in Minneapolis, our last stop. The *North Coast Limited* continued on to Chicago. In May 1971, Amtrak assumed most intercity passenger service, bringing an end to an era of distinctive service on trains like the *North Coast Limited*. For several years Amtrak ran a train over the Northern Pacific route called the *North Coast Hiawatha*, but it was discontinued in 1979, killed by a budget shortfall. Nonetheless, the route of the Northern Pacific survives. Much of it is now used by Burlington Northern Santa Fe and a regional freight carrier, Montana Rail Link. More than a dozen heavy freight trains pass over it every day, and the line also hosts seasonal luxury tour trains. The *North Coast Limited* may be gone, but its memory lives on.

INTRODUCTION

OPPOSITE: *The Central Pacific's locomotive* Jupiter *seen in the great expanse of the Nevada desert west of the Great Salt Lake. While the Central Pacific's greatest feat was conquering the formidable Sierra Nevada in California, it also had to lay track across hundreds of miles of barren, uninhabitable desert. After the turn of the century, much of the CP's original desert crossing was abandoned in favor of a better railroad alignment.*

The American West offered unbridled opportunity to millions of people around the world. Its open plains, awe-inspiring mountains, bountiful wildlife, and unexploited shores were viewed as the panacea for all civilization's evils. The West was the American frontier—millions of acres of unclaimed, unpolluted, unsettled, and uncivilized land. Dreams of the American West inspired men and women to leave their friends, families, and way of life behind in search of a new destiny.

We should never take for granted the strong-spirited pioneer who abandoned all that he or she knew and struck out into the wild unknown in unrelenting pursuit of a better life. It was one thing to contemplate the West; it was quite another to eke out an existence in its unpopulated and often hostile environment. Lack of roads, water, law, and society made survival a daily trial for settlers. Romantic visions of the Great Plains and Rocky Mountains vanished when the prospect of crossing them—on foot—struck the Western pioneers. It was not a land for the faint of heart or weak of spirit. Many who came west were disappointed by the harsh living, and many who attempted to stick it out died before their dreams were realized. Yet, others triumphed in the face of terrible adversity—arid climate, alkaline soil, unrelenting wind, frigid winters, and total lack of basic necessities and comforting amenities. Hostilities with Native Americans and the barbarities of bandits and desperadoes added to the settlers' daily woes.

And, while many who were drawn to the West were moral, hard-working, honest people, others were immoral, wild, opportunistic sorts, who looked to profit through the misfortune of their fellow men.

The first large migration west began in 1849 with the discovery of gold in California by John Sutter. The lure of fast riches

Introduction

drew a youthful lot, many of whom hoped to prosper quickly from easy labor and then return home to the East. In the 1850s, the voyage to California presented a formidable task no matter how it was accomplished. A traveler could go either by land, traversing the vast expanse of the country, or by sea, around the tip of South America, or to the Isthmus of Panama, then overland and continuing by sea to California. All routes were long, expensive, and rife with peril. For widespread settlement of the West to occur, a better way to get there was needed.

Railroads provided a viable, affordable transportation solution. Through the building of railroads, the West was rapidly transformed from a wild frontier to a populated, prosperous part of the United States. At no prior time in history had an area as large as the American West—stretching from the Mississippi River Valley to the Pacific—been settled so rapidly. In a flash, sleepy villages became thriving cities, tiny coastal outposts became bustling ports, and millions of acres of untamed wild prairie became cultivated land. Those already living in the West—the many Native Americans, including the Sioux, the Cheyenne, the Apache—had to make a choice: adjust peacefully or fight. Those who chose to fight fought hard, and with dire consequences. There was no stopping the westward progress, and once the new settlers were established, there was no turning back. The settling of the West was a cultural revolution as well as an agricultural and industrial one.

American railroads had their beginnings on the East Coast during the late 1820s and 1830s. Many considered the rails a novelty at first, but the steam locomotive quickly demonstrated its power. Soon railroads were being built everywhere in the East. Every little hamlet, every town, and every place in between wanted its own railroad line. Any place without a railroad was soon to find that it was no place at all, as railroads replaced primitive roads and canals as the primary arteries of traffic.

In most of the East, population patterns were already established. Railroads were built to connect existing points, usually following the convenient terrain of river valleys and level plains. These lines generally needed few tunnels and only occasionally large bridges. Traffic was concentrated: all along the railroad were the mills, factories, and farms that generated profitable business. From the very beginning the railroads had goods and people to carry. Because railroads made life easier, acceptance of railroad transportation was rapid. It was now faster and easier to

toget where one was going than ever before. A trip that had once taken days now took only a few hours. The primary ingredients that made the steam locomotive go, fuel and water, were abundant. There was no shortage of labor to run the trains, either. And, as the United States established its industrial prowess in the 1840s, there were many firms capable of manufacturing locomotives, iron rails, and other railroad equipment. The railroad infrastructure quickly connected the settled areas of nineteenth-century America, and railroad tracks became as accepted a part of the environment as rivers, lakes, and mountains. Train schedules became part of one's daily ritual, and railroad workers were embraced as upstanding members of most communities.

Railroads of the West followed a different pattern. At first there were few established towns and little originating traffic to be carried between major terminals. The West's geography brought an array of new concerns: wide rivers, towering mountain ranges, and broad, dry deserts to cross. West of Ohio there were no foundries or other major industries. On the plains and in the deserts there were few trees, and basic commodities such as water were scarce or of poor quality. So while the need for a railroad to the Pacific Coast was strong, a practical environment for building one did not exist. More creative methods were needed to coax the rails westward.

OPPOSITE: *Railroad construction often progressed at a rapid pace. Using primitive equipment, animal power, and manual labor, tracks could be laid down across level terrain at a rate of several miles per day.* **ABOVE**: *Scenes like this, concocted to intrigue the public, for the most part did not reflect the reality of Western rail travel. Although very few train riders would ever have viewed this scene from a train window, romantic pictures like this one have tantalized the American imagination for more than a century.*

13

In the East, early railroads were relatively short, often no more than a hundred miles (161km) long. More ambitious railroads—from Albany to Buffalo, for example—could count on traffic along the way to support their construction. If a line did not make it to its proposed destination, it could still rely on traffic from intermediate points to carry it over and generate needed revenue to interest potential investors. As the railroad industry matured, many shorter lines were connected through acquisition, consolidation, and merger to form large trunk lines between major points. By the 1870s, there were four principal trunk lines operating between the East Coast and Chicago. All had been pieced together from smaller companies. For the most part, the West did not enjoy these advantages. A railroad to the Pacific was not going to materialize in the same fashion that railroads in the East had.

Certainly the traffic to and from the West Coast spelled promise, but building a line across two thousand miles (3,218km) of uninhabited territory, much of which was thought at the time to be wasteland, was not financially viable without outside help. Investors viewed promotion schemes to build the early transcontinental lines with considerable skepticism. Who would invest their hard-earned money on a line that might take fifty years to build and another fifty to earn its first dime?

In the 1850s, the distance across the nation seemed incredibly far. To many, building a railroad to the Pacific seemed as difficult as building a line to the moon. The Baltimore & Ohio had projected a line from its home city of Baltimore, Maryland, across the Appalachians to the Ohio River at Wheeling, West Virginia (then still Virginia), in the mid-1820s. Some thirty years later it had just completed its line between those two points. So just imagine how long it might take to build a railroad across the Great American Desert and over the formidable Rocky Mountains! A nice idea, but seriously....

What was needed to get the railroad moving was government backing through grants and subsidy. While private investors were unwilling to gamble on the building of a Pacific railroad, many of those in government knew that such a line was imperative for the future of the United States. It took years of wrangling to come to a satisfactory conclusion, but finally, after strong lobbying by railroad visionaries and promoters, funds were made available through land grants and cash, and the construction of the Pacific Railroad began in 1862, during the Civil War.

While several different routes had been surveyed for the Pacific Railroad, the Central route was ultimately selected as the first line. But even as this line was getting under way, proponents of other lines were gearing up to build. And within thirty years of the Central route's completion, tracks had already spanned several routes throughout the West.

As the railroads grew across the West, so did the population. A site selected as a junction quickly became a town. A campsite for building crews, constructed in haste as the railroad moved west, became a permanent fixture along the right of way when the line was completed. And the lucky wide spot along the tracks selected to be a division point and shop facility soon became a bustling hotbed of economic activity, the envy of surrounding locales. Most towns along the way owed their existence to the railroad. There was

BELOW: *An early map of the Union Pacific, which shows the Central Pacific; Northern Pacific; and Southern Pacific, among other Union Pacific connections and affiliated lines.*

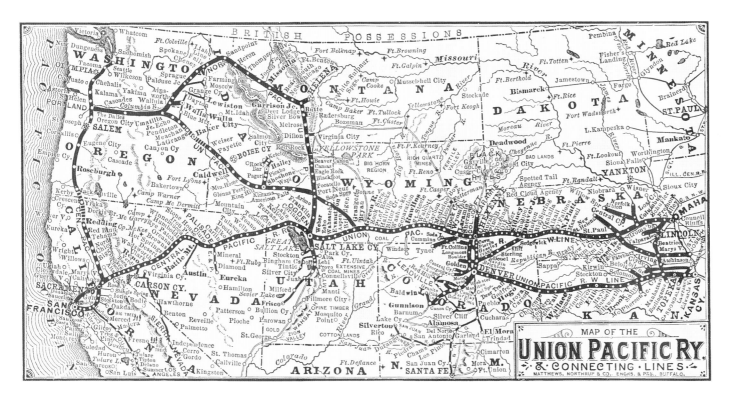

nothing there before the tracks came, and without the railroad, there might be nothing still.

Railroading in the West had its challenges. The nature of the terrain and climate presented railroad operating personnel with a host of problems of a magnitude never imagined in the East. The lack of trees and other materials meant they had to be brought in from great distances. Where grades in the East rarely exceeded 2 percent (a rise of two feet for every hundred traveled horizontally), grades of 3, 4, and even 5 percent were not unheard of in the West. Tunnels through rock walls and towering trestles were required to carry tracks through mountains and over the gorges. Weather, too, was a major problem. Snow so deep as to be unimaginable back East formed tremendous drifts on the plains and closed mountain passes.

Hostile Native Americans posed problems primarily to survey parties and track-laying crews. Once railroads were established and trains were running, relatively few problems were caused by Native Americans.

The remoteness of the West, the absence of civilized society, and an abundance of young, wild, and well-armed individuals led to a problem virtually unheard of in the East: armed train robbery. Bandits, desperadoes, and outlaws first robbed horse-drawn stagecoaches; then, as railroads became a more established mode of transporting goods and wealth, they began robbing trains. The legends of train robbers have long outlasted their brief moment in Western history.

One of the greatest concerns of railroaders and travelers was the danger of wrecks. The lines in the West had their share of major disasters: head-on collisions at high speeds, collapsing bridges, snow blockades, and runaway trains, probably the greatest fear of railroaders operating in the high mountains. If a heavy train's brakes failed, the crew could quickly lose control, with the train careening wildly down a mountainside.

The great distances traversed in the West far exceeded those in the East. Passengers on Eastern lines rarely traveled on a single train for more than a few hours, a day at the most. Western travelers could often expect to ride a single train for days at a time. As a result, the need for sleeping cars and eating accommodations had to be addressed. At first, sleeping cars were relatively crude and the eating establishments worse. But in time, industrious entrepreneurs found more creative solutions to please the weary traveler.

ABOVE: *Santa Fe locomotive No. 5 hauls the company paycar. Obstacles, including livestock that wandered onto the tracks, were often the cause of dangerous and costly wrecks. The cowcatcher—the inclined frame at the front of the locomotive—sweeps such obstructions out of the way.*

Introduction

RIGHT: *This line drawing from 1879, titled* Clear Creek-Cañon "Grundy Bend," *depicts the narrow, forbidding terrain that Western railroad builders faced. Finding a suitable right-of-way was often difficult.*

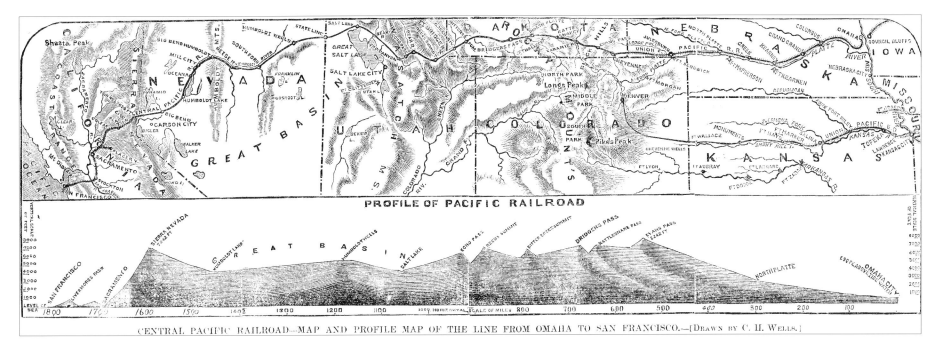

PROFILE OF PACIFIC RAILROAD

CENTRAL PACIFIC RAILROAD—MAP AND PROFILE MAP OF THE LINE FROM OMAHA TO SAN FRANCISCO.—[DRAWN BY C. H. WELLS.]

Spectacular Western scenery, so unlike anything ever seen in the East, in Europe, or anywhere else, offered opportunities for excursions. Bountiful wildlife attracted sportsmen and hunters, and special trains operated exclusively for their benefit. As the tracks were laid and towns were established, agriculture, shipping, and mining interests flourished. Soon freight trains became a common sight throughout the West.

Railroads and railroad building were America's first big businesses, and they attracted all sorts of enterprising individuals: visionaries, investors, financial tycoons, and robber barons. Following the Civil War, the railroads were one of the principal influences on the national economy. When the financing scheme for the Northern Pacific Railroad collapsed in 1873, a nationwide financial panic ensued, the worst ever seen until that time. But when the railroads were booming the economy sailed along with them. Then the most powerful man in America, and probably the world, financier John Pierpont Morgan made his reputation and much of his wealth managing railroad financing. Many of the most famous men of the nineteenth century were linked in one way or another to the railroads, and in the latter half of the century, many of those were Western railroads.

Many of the lines of the West quickly became household names: Union Pacific; Southern Pacific; Northern Pacific; Denver & Rio Grande; and probably the most famous of all, the Atchison, Topeka & Santa Fe. Railroad routes, too, became familiar: the Overland, the Moffat, Donner Pass, and the Sunset. The

trains racing across the western panorama caught the American imagination. Every line had its crack limiteds and expresses. The *Overland Limited*, the *Golden Gate Flyer*, the *North Coast Limited*, and the *Sunset* were some of the great Western passenger trains. Each line tried to outdo its neighbor in offering the latest accommodations and luxuries. Train travel was the state-of-the-art, fashionable, and preferred method of travel. Nowhere was this more true than in the West. Western trains were among the first to carry sleeping cars, observation cars, dining cars, and, in later years, glass-covered Vista Domes. Luxurious limiteds offered every newfangled convenience, often years before they were common elsewhere.

The locomotives in the early days of the West were colorful, brightly decorated affairs. Technologically speaking, they were not substantially different from those found on Eastern lines, but later in the twentieth century, the need for powerful locomotives in the wide-open terrain of the West would result in some of the largest steam locomotives ever built.

Everyone wanted to travel by train, and the railroads took great pleasure in carrying the world's best-known celebrities. Famous actors and actresses, popular generals and statesmen, presidents, Wall Street tycoons, and even foreign royalty all rode the rails. As the West opened up, all wanted to see the sights and explore the West firsthand. The railroad was one of the key ingredients to opening the West and an intrinsic part of its fascination.

ABOVE: *An early grade profile of the Transcontinental Railroad clearly shows that the steepest, toughest part of the line was the Central Pacific's climb up the west slope of the Sierra Nevada to the summit at Donner Pass.*

CHAPTER ONE

THE CENTRAL PACIFIC

❧

OPPOSITE: *The Central Pacific's Falcon leads a federal inspection train over a recently completed portion of the railroad. The Central Pacific and Union Pacific were given cash awards by the federal government for each mile of completed railroad.*

THEODORE JUDAH AND THE BIG FOUR

One inspired visionary played an instrumental role in the building of the Pacific Railroad. He fought against all odds in pursuit of his dream. Plying many talents, wearing many hats, traveling to all corners of the nation, he pulled together the resources to push a railroad across the formidable Sierra Nevada and ultimately across the entire American West. And, unfortunately, this one man would never see or ride a train clear across the United States. Theodore D. Judah was this visionary.

Judah was born in Bridgeport, Connecticut, in 1826, at the dawn of the railroad age. He focused his talents on engineering at a young age, working on a variety of significant transportation projects, including the Erie Canal—the legendary waterway connecting with the Hudson River at Albany, New York, allowing passage down to New York City—making his mark as an engineering talent. In quick succession, Judah worked on several railroad projects in the East. He served as assistant engineer for the Troy & Schenectady Railroad; and he was the chief engineer for the Buffalo and New York Railroad; but Judah made his reputation with his clever engineering of a line through the treacherous

Niagara Gorge. Upon completing that job—well ahead of schedule—Judah had his choice of positions. The one that intrigued him the most was that of chief engineer for the Sacramento Valley Railroad in distant California.

Early in his career Theodore Judah married Anna Pierce, who traveled with him on his journeys west. Their romantic marriage held together through great adversity, and after Theodore's death, Anna would chronicle his life's achievements. Many women might not have taken to the idea of abandoning their homes and family to follow their husband to the wilds of California, but Anna did. Had she not, the railroad to the Pacific might have been delayed by decades until another capable visionary happened along to drive it through. Because without Anna, it's doubtful that Theodore would have remained in California long enough to finish the project he had been hired for, let alone take on the quest of his life—the Pacific Railroad. Furthermore, it is doubtful that anyone else would have had all the skills necessary to complete this strategic link when Judah did. Ultimately, a railroad would have been built anyway, but Judah encouraged its construction on all fronts, greatly accelerating its completion.

Theodore and Anna arrived in Sacramento in 1854, less than six years after the discovery of gold near John Sutter's mill had sent men from around the world dashing for the Sierra Nevada. A boomtown, with muddy streets and hastily constructed shacks masquerading as buildings, Sacramento was no Emerald City. But Judah was not seeking comfort, and he put his talents to work on the Sacramento Valley line. It would be the first railroad in California, a line designed to connect the growing inland port with the mining towns in the Sierra foothills. He did his job well, but soon felt his energy drawn to the towering summits on the eastern horizon. Sacramento was anything but a mountain town; it sat squarely in the great Central Valley. But on a clear day the Sierra loomed ominously like a forbidding wall over the gold rush town. Even before he had finished his required duties with the Sacramento Valley, Judah began exploring the Sierra. The idea of a railroad east over these mountains burned within him like a fever. The germ that bit him had hit others as well, but Judah had the verve and talent to take on this impossible dream. He was able to find support, though at times it proved elusive. The federal government recognized the strategic value of a Pacific railroad. Furthermore, many Californians had the desire for a railroad—though few of them really believed that one could be built.

For Judah, the Pacific Railroad was a big puzzle. Most of the pieces were available to him; he just needed to find out how they fit together. The first piece, that of locating a viable right-of-way, was perhaps the easiest. Railroad engineering was his trade; he had built railroads in impossible places before. Yet even those first steps had their challenges. To untrained eyes, the mountains looked like one jagged rock wall after another, separated only by deep precipices, towering trees, and the occasional snow-crested ridge. But Judah sought a path. He spent months in the mountains with Anna, surveying a route. Few men before him had done much work in securing a right-of-way in these mountains, and much of his survey was original. Theodore and Anna made more than twenty trips into the mountains, surveying the land and looking for the future railroad's right-of-way. And even before he had finished his surveys and located a route for the railroad—Judah had difficulty finding a suitable pass through the mountains at the summit—he began fueling his propaganda machine to drum up financial support.

He enlisted the aid of the *Sacramento Union*, a newspaper whose editor became an ardent supporter of the Pacific Railroad. Judah wrote persuasive editorials for the paper, singing the song of the railroad. In 1857 he published and distributed a Pacific Railroad Plan, making sure that every influential government official—including the president—received a copy. In 1859 he helped arrange a Pacific Railroad convention in San Francisco, attempting to recruit backers for his railroad. Certainly there was interest, but interest alone did not provide capital, and few believed the project's viability merited investment. Despite Judah's surveys, speeches, and editorials, the prospect of a railroad over the Sierra still seemed absurd.

Undaunted, Judah went to Washington in autumn 1859 and set up a Pacific Railroad Museum in the Capitol Building and lobbied both Congress and the president. The United States were on the brink of civil war, and tensions were high over issues of slavery and sectionalism, so Judah appealed to the feelings of the time. He promoted the railroad as good for the Union, stressing the benefits of settling the "Great American Desert." Essentially, Judah wanted the allocation of land and the federal guarantee of railroad bonds to help attract investors. He had support, but not enough, and Judah did not receive the attention he had hoped for. The legislators were too distracted by the growing crisis between Northern and Southern states to pay Judah's railroad much attention. Despite endorsement by the California legislature, Judah's bill before Congress was pushed aside.

Discouraged but still adamant in his vision, Judah returned to California to continue the fight. In the meantime, the nation erupted into full-blown civil war. Drawn back to the mountains in October 1859, Judah met with Daniel Strong, a druggist at the mining town of Dutch Flat, and, more important, an amateur surveyor and Pacific Railroad proponent. Strong believed he had found the Sierra crossing that Judah had been searching for. Indeed he had, and Judah soon surveyed the narrow ridge of land rising between the American and Yuba river canyons. This was the missing link in the railroad's right-of-way. His earlier surveys had fallen apart as the railroad reached the summit. But with this route, the railroad would be able to cross the mountains on a relatively straight path with minimal tunneling. In a few places, such as Blue Canyon, the railroad would have to wind in at one level, circle around, and climb out at a higher point in order to maintain a steady grade. There was the need for some serious tunneling at the railroad's summit, the legendary Donner Pass, but this route was economically viable; Judah knew he could build a railroad here.

Encouraged by this great find, Judah worked out cost estimates and personally drafted the needed paperwork to create the Central Pacific Railroad. Daniel Strong gladly purchased stock from Judah, agreeing to help him sell more, and the great Pacific Railroad was under way. Survey in hand, Judah went to San Francisco, the financial epicenter of California, hopeful that he could attract investors. To encourage skeptical investors, Judah argued that even if his railroad was only completed across the mountains to the silver mines of Nevada, lucrative silver traffic would produce healthy revenue for years to come. However, when the railroad was finally completed across the nation, its profits would soar even higher.

Judah believed passionately in his railroad; he was convinced that the following year Congress would pass the needed legislation to enable construction, and that rails would soon be laid over the mountains. Judah's conviction did not persuade San Francisco investors—perhaps his personality did not instill confidence, or maybe his idea did not appeal to those with money—but after several months of hustling, he realized that funding would have to be raised elsewhere. So in December 1860 he went to Sacramento, where he had landed six years earlier, to seek investors. He would not rest; his railroad had so much promise, it had to be built.

While Judah struggled to convince investors in California—his charts, surveys, and railroad schemes giving his peers cause to question his sanity—the Pacific Railroad was receiving considerable support in the East, where politicians valued the project. In December 1860, Judah's fortune took a turn for the better. Congress passed the Curtis Bill, legislation mandating the construction of the Pacific Railroad. Furthermore, President-elect Lincoln, who would soon take office, was an ardent supporter of a Pacific Railroad. Other political events aided Judah as well. One of the reasons support for the Pacific Railroad had stalled in Washington was the ongoing debate over a northern versus a southern route for the line. North and South were divided over which route to build on, each preferring the route most likely to aid their cause, and no progress was made. When South Carolina seceded from the Union, followed by other Southern states, it made Congress' selection of a northern route possible. Then, in January 1861, a crucial meeting occurred, one that would finally let Judah's railroad take off.

The Big Four

Following another unsuccessful promotional meeting in Sacramento, Judah was approached by two Sacramento businessmen, Collis Potter Huntington and Mark Hopkins. Where others had dismissed Judah, these men took him seriously. They recognized the potential of his railroad and saw the money that could be made from it. Several days later, Judah met with Huntington and Hopkins along with several other successful members of the Sacramento business community, including Leland Stanford and Charles Crocker. These four men had acquired small fortunes by running respectable businesses during the volatile times following the California gold rush. There were other businessmen at that fateful meeting, and though seven of them originally agreed to back Judah, it was Huntington, Hopkins, Stanford, and Crocker that would run the enterprise and build the railroad. Collectively known as the "Big Four," these men soon became the most important force in California railroading for four decades to follow. The Big Four took Judah's idea and pushed it to completion, then proceeded to build and operate railroads throughout California and the West.

Huntington, a man of impeccable business savvy and strong constitution, provided brains for the quartet. He was the most instrumental figure, and the longest lived of the Big Four. Born to poor parents at Harwington, Connecticut, in October 1821, Huntington was taught thrift at a very early age—a lesson that proved valuable in his long business career. As a young man he regularly endured hard exercise; as an old man he boasted of his endurance. His health and strength were exceptional. Early on he experimented with a variety of business ventures, tackling each one with success. In 1849 he was bitten by the gold bug and traveled to California in search of his fortune. While he may be considered a Forty-niner, Huntington had not anticipated becoming a gold miner. Instead he viewed California as the ultimate business opportunity. As Oscar Lewis notes in his book *The Big Four*: "Few adventurers who set out for the gold field were less affected than he by the prevailing attitude of improvidence and specious optimism."

In business, Huntington was an opportunist, but not a gambler. He believed in earning his keep through brains and brawn. Never one to miss a good business opportunity, en route west Huntington postponed his eventual prosperity in California to earn a small fortune in Nicaragua. He bought and sold goods there, careful to earn a handsome profit with every transaction. He arrived in California with a decent sum, unlike many of those seeking golden bounty, who arrived nearly penniless. Once established in Sacramento, he quickly garnered respect in the business community. He sold nonperishable goods and excelled at his trade by carefully observing the laws of supply and demand. Lewis relates Huntington's philosophy: "I kept my warehouse full when prices were low, and when they went up, I sold out."

Business aside, Huntington conducted his personal life with propriety. A strict teetotaler, he refrained from all varieties of wanton carousing, often retiring in the early evening. He insisted that his employees conduct themselves in a similar fashion—notable in Sacramento, a town rife with gambling, drinking, and prostitution. Throughout his life Huntington remained a private person, had few close friends, and shunned public life.

Leland Stanford was a large man. His manner and speech were slow, cautious, and deliberate. In marked contrast to Huntington, he was genial, vain, and prone to ostentatious display. Where Huntington preferred to work quietly in the shadows, Stanford was the Big Four's public persona, and his political appetite thrust him into the limelight. For thirty years he acted as president of the railroad, often appearing at public events, while Huntington quietly dominated the railroad's business affairs. Stanford's aspirations went beyond his duty to the railroad: in 1862 he was elected governor of California, and in the 1880s he served as senator. Huntington, on the other hand, was content to develop the railroad as the greatest power in California.

One of eight children, Stanford was born at Watervliet, New York, in March 1824. His railroad experience came early; as a teenager he earned his keep by chopping wood for one of the local railroads. But he did not labor long. His father decided that of the eight children, Leland should be educated, and so he attended school in Utica and later in Syracuse. He never graduated, but put his learning to good use by joining an Albany law firm. After three years he was admitted to the New York Bar. Although ambition brought him to the frontier, while others were migrating to California, Stanford married and moved to Port Washington, Wisconsin, to practice law. This ended in disaster: a fire destroyed his business along with part of the town. He returned to Albany disillusioned and decided to try California. Some of his brothers had gone there to do business, so Leland joined them, arriving in San Francisco in 1852. He viewed California as a means toward the rapid accumulation of fortune, not as a lifelong residence. His wife, Jane, had chosen to remain in the East with her parents and wait for him. So after three years of managing his brothers' successful Sacramento grocery, he returned to Albany. But he could not resist the allure of California so easily. Stanford found the pace of Eastern living not to his liking; he realized that his destiny lay in California. His wife, too, was bored with Albany, and with her he returned to Sacramento. On his return to California he enjoyed success in the grocery business and took an interest in the fledgling California Republican Party, where he met his future business partners.

Later in life, after he came to revel in his success, he modeled himself after European aristocracy and expected appropriate treatment from others. He had several opulent mansions built for himself and his wife. Oscar Lewis said that Stanford's house atop Nob Hill in San Francisco "dominated the city like the castle of a medieval hill town." The Stanfords enjoyed traveling around the railroad in their luxurious private car, *Stanford*. As they passed by stations along the way, employees were expected to stand at attention and salute their president. Undoubtedly, Huntington found this arrogant and pompous behavior highly annoying and distasteful.

Beyond the railroad and politics, Stanford enjoyed several extravagant pursuits. He bred racehorses in a self-styled effort to improve the quality of the animal in California. When this began to bore him, he turned to wine. Stanford wished for California to replace France as the leading producer of quality wines, and

he purchased more than fifty thousand acres in the northern Sacramento Valley for his vineyards. This resulted in a complete failure when the climate refused to cooperate. One of his last pursuits, and his most enduring personal legacy, stemmed from the tragic death of his only son, Leland Stanford, Jr., from typhoid fever. To honor his son, Stanford created a world-class university at Palo Alto.

Charlie Crocker left power jockeying to Huntington and Stanford, and assumed the role of Central Pacific's chief builder. At this, he excelled. Biographer Oscar Lewis describes him as "boastful, stubborn, tactless, vain, and completely lacking in the quality then described as low cunning."

He was just the man to get out on the ground and get the job done. In the early stages he was a doer, not a talker, and he personally oversaw the construction of the railroad to Promontory, spending more time along the line than at home. He often boasted of his exploits walking the line he built over Donner Pass: "Why, I used to go up and down the road in my car like a mad bull, stopping along where there was anything going amiss and raising old Nick. The men were afraid because I was just looking for something to find fault with."

Like the others, Crocker was a transplanted Easterner. He was born in Troy, New York, in 1822 and migrated west during the gold rush. Once in California, he quickly concluded that he was not suited to gold mining, and instead became a merchant, opening a store. His business eventually relocated to Sacramento, and like Huntington and Stanford, he joined the Republican Party in 1856. By 1860 his dry goods store was a thriving, substantial part of the Sacramento business community, and he was serving his first term in the California Legislature.

Following the completion of the Pacific Railroad in 1869, Crocker settled into a more passive role, choosing to relax and enjoy his wealth. He built an enormous Victorian mansion in San Francisco, where he lived until his death in 1888.

The senior member of the Big Four, and the most level-headed of the group, was Mark Hopkins, often known simply as "Uncle Mark." He was born at Henderson, New York, in

BELOW: "Uncle" Mark Hopkins was the oldest of the Big Four, and the most conservative. Before they became involved in railroading, Huntington and Hopkins operated a successful hardware business in Sacramento. BELOW LEFT: Charlie Crocker played an active role in the construction of the Central Pacific.

THE *C. P. HUNTINGTON*

One of the best known and most loved Southern Pacific steam locomotives is the diminutive *C. P. Huntington*. It was a single-driver tank engine with a 4-2-4 wheel arrangement (four guiding wheels, followed by one pair of driving wheels and four wheels trailing). Although the *C. P. Huntington* was actually Central Pacific's third locomotive, it was given the distinctive number "1" as an honor to Collis Porter Huntington, one of Central Pacific's "Big Four," and the locomotive's namesake. An ornate product of the Victorian era, it was built by the Cooke Locomotive Works (also known as Danforth, Cooke & Company) of Paterson, New Jersey, in 1863. It was shipped to California by way of Cape Horn

ABOVE: The *C. P. Huntington* was the third locomotive owned by the Central Pacific. It was restored in 1915 for the Panama-Pacific Expo and now resides at the California State Railroad Museum in Sacramento. RIGHT: Built by the Cooke Locomotive Works in 1863, the *C. P. Huntington* was shipped to California from the East via sailing ship around Cape Horn at the tip of South America. After its restoration in 1914, the locomotive became a celebrity and a symbol of the Southern Pacific.

on the vessel *Success*. To the casual observer this single-driver locomotive might appear curiously small, the sort of locomotive found on pink-and-blue wallpaper in a children's nursery and not one for any practical purpose. While the 4-4-0 American-type locomotive with its two sets of drivers has received greater recognition, single-driver locomotives also experienced some popularity in the United States prior to 1870. This type of locomotive was not unique; Central Pacific owned several of them.

In its original form, the *C. P. Huntington* did not have a headlight and was prohibited from service at night. Later it was modified: a headlight was added, supported by decorative iron brackets, and its balloon smokestack was replaced by a stack of the diamond variety more commonly found on Central Pacific locomotives. After serving as a construction locomotive, used to build the Central Pacific crossing of Donner Pass, it was transferred to another Big Four property, the Southern Pacific. The little engine spent much of its active life in the Bay Area hauling short passenger

trains for Southern Pacific and affiliated companies. In the 1890s, it was demoted to less glamorous duties, and in 1897 it was converted, ignobly, to a weed burner. About the time of C. P. Huntington's death in 1900, the locomotive was retired and sentenced to scrapping. Its historical significance and diminutive stature inspired sentiment in the shop employees at Sacramento, where the locomotive was to be dismantled. They tucked the locomotive away,

rather than reducing it to scrap. In 1914 the Southern Pacific decided to restore the historic engine for display at the 1915 Panama Exposition in San Francisco. That grand affair elevated the *C. P. Huntington* to celebrity status. It was exhibited widely and restored to steam for a few years in the 1920s and 1930s. Today it is proudly displayed at the California State Railroad Museum in Sacramento.

Another Central Pacific locomotive, built to nearly identical specifications as the *C. P. Huntington*, was named for visionary Theodore D. Judah. Like Judah, who died at age thirty-seven, six years before the railroad was completed, the *T. D. Judah* came to a premature demise. It was first modified, then disposed of in 1889. While the *C. P. Huntington* became a symbol of the Southern Pacific, the *T. D. Judah* is hardly remembered.

OPPOSITE: *The Central Pacific route through the California Sierra traverses some of the most awe-inspiring scenery in the West. Here, an eastbound train pauses near Cape Horn, east of Colfax, California, on its ascent to Donner Pass. Between Colfax and Emigrant Gap, the Central Pacific route follows the edge of the American River Canyon—in some places the tracks are two thousand feet (609.6m) above the river.*

September 1813, and was engaged in a number of professions, including law, before moving to California during the gold rush. Hopkins and his two dozen companions were intent on gold mining but abandoned the notion once they arrived. The prospects for mining had been greatly exaggerated, so Hopkins chose to open a general store instead. In 1856 he went into business with Huntington, a partnership that proved long and fruitful for both men.

Among the Big Four, Hopkins served calmly as the accountant, rarely leaving the office. He took the time to carefully pore over the details of business matters. He was equally respected by the other members and often mediated disagreements. Huntington once said of Uncle Mark, "[H]e was one of the truest and best men that ever lived." He also noted, "I never considered anything finished until Hopkins looked at it."

The Railroad Building Begins

Soon the Big Four, along with Judah, Strong, and several other investors, had formally chartered the Central Pacific. In June 1861, they held elections. Stanford became president, Huntington vice president, and Judah chief engineer. They needed to complete Judah's surveying, and financed the effort. Thrilled with the prospect that the railroad was finally under way, Judah variously brought Huntington, Stanford, and Crocker to the Sierra to inspect his crossing. Not entirely satisfied, Huntington demanded that other routes still be investigated. So he and Judah spent part of the summer in the deep and narrow Feather River Canyon located to the north of Donner Pass and inspected that route in combination with the crossing at Beckworth Pass. The territory traversed by the lower Feather River Canyon was so treacherous that no road had even been built along it. In some places sheer rock walls rose hundreds of feet high, and there was no place to stand, let alone build a railroad line. Thirty or forty tunnels would be needed, and the cost of building a line through the canyon was deemed prohibitive. Huntington acquiesced to the Donner Pass crossing Judah had selected. The rest of the season was spent completing the survey as planned.

Armed with the Big Four's financial support and a completed survey, Judah returned to Washington in the autumn of 1861 to lobby for his railroad and subscribe stockholders. Huntington

followed that winter. Judah's thorough knowledge of railroading paid off. He was a very convincing proponent and worked directly with congressmen to draft legislation to support construction of his railroad. The result was the Pacific Railroad Act of 1862, an idea whose time had come. The Senate and House both passed it in June 1862, and shortly thereafter President Lincoln's signature made it a law.

Two companies were to build the line, one working east to west from Omaha, Nebraska, the other west to east from Sacramento. The Central Pacific was specifically designated as the western company. A new company to be known as the Union Pacific was to build the eastern portion. Subsidies were provided in the form of land grants and predetermined dollar amounts for each mile of line completed. There were three different amounts of subsidy, depending on the nature of the land to be crossed. The subsidy for building through the mountains was three times higher than for building across gentle terrain. This difference in subsidies later caused a deep rift between Judah and the Big Four.

Soon after Judah returned from Washington, he and the Big Four began to have differences over how the railroad's affairs should be handled. John Hoyt Williams illustrates some of the disparities between them in his book *A Great and Shining Road*. Judah—motivated by his vision for the railroad rather than by economics—believed the Central Pacific should have a grand office in Sacramento and designed a $12,000 brick building for that purpose. His plan, however, was rejected by the board and replaced—on Huntington's orders—with a $150 shack. Judah also had qualms about matters of construction and the business methods the Big Four employed. Williams relates:

> ...*plans for actual construction were discussed and debated. Crocker, who had bossed a small iron foundry in Indiana for a while, felt himself a capable construction boss. This Judah openly doubted, but supported by the rest of the Big Four, Crocker drew up a contract for constructing the first eighteen miles....Over Judah's and Bailey's protests, the Charles Crocker Contracting Company was awarded the first stretch of road two days after Christmas [1862], and two days after Crocker resigned from the board (keeping his stock of course), to avoid charges of conflict of interest. His place on the board was taken by a new investor, his brother, E. B. [Crocker], who had recently*

CENTRAL PACIFIC NO. 1: THE *GOVERNOR STANFORD*

Imagine the excitement in Sacramento, California, on October 26, 1863, when the first locomotive for the Pacific Railroad arrived. Years of discussion had finally resulted in action. Naysayers had decried the impassioned Theodore Judah as crazy, but on July 2, 1862, President Abraham Lincoln had signed the Pacific Railroad Act, and now a year later, the railroad's first locomotive was ready for service. Central Pacific No. 1, the *Governor Stanford*, was a glorious Victorian machine named for Leland Stanford, Civil War Governor of California and one of the Big Four, who served as the railroad's first president. It cost the tremendous sum of fourteen thousand dollars—the Civil War had driven up the price of new locomotives, and they cost nearly twice as much as before the war. The cost of shipping the locomotive to California was also quite significant.

There were other problems as well. When Central Pacific ordered the locomotive from R. Norris & Son in Philadelphia, the gauge of the Pacific Railroad was to be the California standard, five feet (152cm). The *Governor Stanford* was constructed as ordered, but by the time it arrived, the gauge of the Pacific Railroad had been changed to the national standard—4 feet, 8½ inches (143cm)—and the locomotive had to be regauged.

More than two weeks after its arrival, Central Pacific put the *Governor Stanford* under steam, and crowds flocked to see it. Its debut had been planned for November 9, but problems with the engine's valves delayed the first trip. While it had been constructed in Pennsylvania, it was shipped in pieces and required final assembly in California.

In many ways a typical American-type locomotive, the *Governor Stanford* made for an impressive sight to the throngs of people anticipating its performance. More than 50 feet (15m) long, the locomotive sported a pair of 4½-foot (137cm) driving wheels painted bright red with a gold star accenting the hubs. Its tender, cab, and head lamp (a large ornate box with a kerosene lamp surrounded by a parabolic reflector) were painted a sharp maroon with gold accents. The window frames were bright yellow and the siderods, piston casings, steam dome, and bell were made of highly polished brass that glistened in the California sun. The *Governor Stanford* stood as a symbol of the Pacific Railroad, continued prosperity, and ease of transportation. Although the rails of the Central Pacific had not yet left the city limits, and both the summit of Donner Pass and the even more distant connection with the Union Pacific were still years away, proud officials of the fledgling railroad ran the *Governor Stanford* back and forth on the short section of completed track to celebrate the beginning of what was certain to become a prosperous and historic rail line. Soon afterward this first locomotive was pressed into service building the railroad. In later years the locomotive found use as the Sacramento shop switcher and did a stint as a fire engine in service on a water train, but it was seldom used for the more glamorous tasks reserved for newer and more powerful locomotives. In 1899 the railroad rehabilitated the *Governor Stanford* and gave it to Stanford University. It now resides along with a host of other historically significant California locomotives at the California State Railroad Museum in Sacramento.

ABOVE: The Central Pacific's first locomotive, the *Governor Stanford*, entered service on November 10, 1863. A product of R. Norris & Son, it cost the railroad about fourteen thousand dollars. OPPOSITE: Named after Leland Stanford, the first president of the Central Pacific Railroad, the *Governor Stanford* is now displayed at the California State Railroad Museum in Sacramento.

ABOVE: *The Central Pacific was built with picks and shovels and black powder. Yet, despite a complete lack of sophisticated technology, the railroad was completed over Donner Pass in less than five years.*

been appointed the company's attorney. He had also—hardly coincidentally—just been named interim chief justice of the California Supreme Court, by the company's president, Governor Leland Stanford.

On January 8, 1863, Governor Stanford was among the dignitaries who presided over the Central Pacific's groundbreaking ceremonies. It was a day of festivity—the long-talked-about Pacific Railroad would finally begin construction. Speeches were made, a brass band played, and crowds cheered. George Kraus

relays the *Sacramento Union* report of January 9 in his book *High Road to Promontory*:

> *Two wagons loaded with earth were driven up in front of the rostrum, and Governor Stanford, with a zeal and athletic vigor that showed his heart was in the work and his muscle in the right place, seized the shovel, and amid cheering of the crowd deposited the first earth for the embankment. The enthusiastic Charles Crocker promptly called for "nine cheers" and the crowd, sharing his enthusiasm, cheeringly responded. The sun smiled brightly, and everybody felt happy because, after so many years of dreaming, scheming, talking and toiling, they saw with their own eyes the actual commencement of a Pacific Railroad....*

The irony in this glowing prose was that the principal dreamer, schemer, talker, and toiler, Theodore Judah, was not smiling. He had serious reservations about the Big Four's intentions. Their construction shenanigans alarmed and infuriated him. He began to doubt whether they really intended to build "his" railroad, or just planned to profit from the construction.

The issue of where the mountains began became a focal point of Judah's dissatisfaction with construction methods and the Big Four's business practice. Judah believed the mountains began at one point, the Big Four insisted they began at another, and the difference between their judgments had substantial implications. Each mile in the mountains meant thousands of dollars in additional federal subsidies to the fledgling railroad. The Big Four looked at the matter in financial terms, and because they could earn greater subsidy by building a line in the mountains, they had every incentive to find the mountains closer to Sacramento. In fact, they decided the mountains began at what appeared to be level terrain, a location called Arcade Creek, some seven miles (11km) east of Sacramento. Crocker even had an expert geologist, Professor J. D. Whitney, verify this. This action confirmed Judah's fears about the Big Four. He began to question their motives and their morality.

While the Big Four used dubious means to raise capital, they had reason for concern. Despite federal endorsement, the railroad suffered from severe financial problems. Judah had vastly underestimated construction costs, and, furthermore, stock sales were pitiful. Critics continued to lambaste the Pacific Railroad publicly.

Williams writes that Judah, with his high-principled ideals, lacked a realistic approach for raising adequate funds to build the line. He sincerely believed in "his" railroad and assumed that others would too, and that they would invest the needed dollars to build it. He was continually baffled when investor support failed to materialize, and was appalled when the Big Four used questionable means to drum up funds and support.

The Big Four saw Judah as a thorn in their sides. He had already accomplished what they needed him to do, and now they wanted him out. First they tried to force him out; when that failed, they bought him out. Judah was not just going to bow out of the railroad he had fought so hard for. He would not let the unabashed greed of Sacramento merchants and would-be railroad magnates undermine his dream. He had brought the Big Four in, and if he had to, he would force them out.

In October 1863, Judah and Anna boarded a ship headed for New York City, where Judah intended to raise the capital necessary to buy out the Big Four. This dream quickly became a nightmare. Crossing Panama he contracted a tropical fever; he died shortly after his arrival in New York. Meanwhile, the railroad was finally under way: the first rails were laid and progress was being made. In a few years, despite Judah's fears, his Pacific Railroad was completed. Today a mountain at the summit bears his name, and the railroad remains his living legacy.

HOW COLFAX WAS NAMED

Just above an elevation of twenty-two hundred feet (671m) on the western slope of the California Sierra, some fifty miles (80km) west of the summit at Donner Pass, was a plot of relatively level ground. Here, high above the American River, surrounded by towering evergreens and thick-stemmed, small-leafed manzanita bushes, was Illinoistown. In the summer of 1865, this bustling boomtown was home to both Irish and Chinese railroad workers. It was near "end of track" on the Central Pacific's construction on the transcontinental route. More than a year of construction had brought the tracks up to the edge of Long Ravine, and the railroad's real climb through the mountains was still ahead.

A team of celebrities touring the West—the Honorable Schuyler Colfax, a six-term congressman from Indiana and Speaker of the House of Representatives; Samuel Bowles of the Springfield, Massachusetts, *Republican*; William Bross of the *Chicago Tribune*; and Bert Richardson of the *New York Tribune*— had reached California just as Central Pacific engineers were

ABOVE LEFT: *Several locomotives and crews pose for a photographic portrait at a location believed to be Ogden, Utah. The Union Pacific–Central Pacific transcontinental route bypassed Salt Lake City, instead passing through Ogden several miles farther north.* **ABOVE RIGHT:** *In 1865, career politician Schuyler Colfax—then a congressman from Indiana and Speaker of the House—was given a celebrity tour of the Central Pacific construction in the California Sierra. Illinoistown was renamed in his honor.*

ABOVE: *Central Pacific's* Nevada *poses at Colfax, California. Colfax was an important railroad town where the railroad added extra locomotives called "helpers" to heavy trains climbing eastward toward Donner Pass.*

working the railroad grade east of Illinoistown. Always in the company of a military escort, the distinguished visitors had been experiencing the wonders of Wild Western living first-hand. Earlier in the summer they had inspected progress (or lack thereof) on the Union Pacific in Nebraska and Wyoming; in so doing, they came dangerously close on several occasions to being attacked by warring Native Americans. Apparently a Mormon wagon train was attacked nearly within eyesight of the Easterners' stagecoach. Yet not all of their pursuits risked bodily harm. In his book *A Great and Shining Road*, John Hoyt Williams relates that when the party reached Denver, Ben Holiday, "The Stagecoach King," loaned Colfax his new Concord coach. Colfax reportedly toured in posh style, stopping along the way to fish and hunt. Whether Colfax himself partook in Holiday's fully stocked bar is questionable; it is reported that the Speaker preferred cigars to alcohol.

Central Pacific president Leland Stanford, whose gift for publicity and political favoritism rarely failed him, invited Colfax and company to inspect his railroad. Colfax, already a hardy proponent of the Pacific Railroad (and likely an early railroad

enthusiast), jumped at the opportunity. Stanford brought his guests on a first-class tour of the property; they observed the wonders of the great railroad's construction—trestles, fills, and deep rock cuts. Richardson, intrigued by the Chinese workmen, marveled about their great number, workmanship, and curious customs in articles he wrote for the *New York Tribune* back East. On arriving at the end of track, Stanford, in a politically savvy move, changed the name of Illinoistown to Colfax in honor of his guest. Schuyler Colfax, known to many as "Smiler" for his amiability and pleasant expression, was quite pleased. Lucius Beebe, in his book on the Central Pacific and Southern Pacific, speculates (with some sarcasm) that after Colfax aroused the attention of the Central Pacific's workers (presumably the Irish ones), "[t]he enchanted railroaders couldn't wait to pour from the community's wealth of saloons to tear down the markers which said Illinoistown and put up hastily painted signs proclaiming it as Colfax." Stanford, Colfax, and company continued past the newly christened town and moved on horseback up toward the summit.

Representative Colfax went on to become vice president of the United States under Ulysses S. Grant. The town bearing his

LEFT: *Building and operating a railroad in the desert was a very difficult business. A lack of water was one problem. In this picture, what appears to be a Central Pacific water train crosses the Nevada desert near Humboldt Lake.*

name became an important station along the transcontinental railroad. It became a helper base—where extra locomotives called "helpers" were added to assist heavy eastbound trains assaulting the steep mountain grades.

For many years trains called "water trains" or "fire trains" were stationed on Donner Pass to protect the railroad from wildfires. In the dry season, sparks from locomotives had a tendency to ignite brushfires along the right-of-way. The railroad positioned special trains at several locations on Donner Pass to protect its property. At higher elevations these trains were especially valued for protecting the many miles of wooden snowsheds, which often caught fire in the summer months. The fire trains consisted of several tank cars full of water, equipped with high-pressure hoses, and a specially assigned locomotive equipped with a water pump. Originally the tank cars were made of wood and carried more than seven thousand gallons (26,495l) of water each. The water trains sat at key points along the line, ready on a moment's notice to respond to a distress signal. Author Gerald M. Best describes how one of these fire trains saved Colfax on a hot summer night in 1887:

> *The Colfax Hotel caught fire and the sparks from the burning buildings were carried on a high wind, setting fires north and south of the Central Pacific tracks. The Blue Canyon fire train made a fast run to Colfax, saving the roundhouse, depot and freight house, all of which were in the path of the fire. Checking the spread of the fire through the wooden buildings of the town, [the fire train and its crew] were credited with having prevented the almost complete destruction of the village.*

Today Colfax retains much of its character and remains an important station on the Donner Pass crossing. Amtrak's *California Zephyr* still calls on the Colfax depot—making it one of the smaller towns to retain regular passenger service. Helpers are still occasionally based here to assist the never-ending parade of heavy eastbound freights climbing Donner Pass.

THE GOLDEN SPIKE

The legendary Golden Spike ceremony was a synchronized—although largely unrehearsed—public event marking one of the most significant moments in transportation history: the joining of the Union Pacific and Central Pacific railroads at Promontory, Utah. The ceremonial golden spike was a symbol of unity, of completion, of a better nation and a better world. The Pacific Railroad—more than a decade in the making—was ready for business. East and West were joined by iron rails. The trip to the Pacific, once an adventure endured by only the most rugged travelers, was now open to nearly everyone.

The building of this railroad, one of the great sagas of the nineteenth century, was a classic struggle of man against man, and man against nature. The sheer magnitude of the project had no real parallel in the United States. It represented millions of hours of work and tens of thousands of people working for years. The building of the Pacific Railroad was a truly amazing accomplishment. It was built with relatively crude tools in a relatively

LOCOMOTIVES OF THE GOLDEN SPIKE

Thrust from their routine duties into the limelight, two common locomotives of the 1860s became two of the best-known locomotives in the United States, and quite possibly in the world.

Perhaps the most widely reproduced image in railroading is A. J. Russell's famous portrait of Central Pacific's *Jupiter* and Union Pacific's No. 119 meeting, pilot to pilot, at Promontory, Utah, on May 10, 1869. Historian John H. White, Jr., argues convincingly that these two locomotives are among the most familiar to Americans. Now more than 125 years after that crucial event, the sort of locomotive pictured, the standard 4-4-0 American type, remains the railroad locomotive still most familiar to Americans. Granted, many other examples of the American type help reinforce this image, the *General* of Civil War fame being one, along with a number of locomotives highlighted in this book. Some twenty-five thousand American-type locomotives were constructed, more than most other types of engine.

Ironically, neither *Jupiter* nor Union Pacific's No. 119 were the locomotives intended for the ceremony at Promontory. Central Pacific's *Antelope*, a particularly fine locomotive built by McKay & Aldus and dandied up especially for the occasion, was damaged en route and spent May 10, 1869, awaiting repair at the Wadsworth, Nevada, shop. Union Pacific's intended locomotive was unable to attend because a washout stranded it many miles east of the celebration. Substitutes took the places designed for the railroad's best. These were common locomotives of the period: *Jupiter*, a nearly new product of the Schenectady Locomotive Works intended for fast passenger trains, and No. 119, a standard type built by the Rogers Locomotive Works for freight service on Union Pacific.

Standard, mundane locomotives were used at the famous Golden Spike ceremony? Standard, yes; mundane, hardly. The common locomotive of these Victorian times was, by modern thought, outright indulgent in its decor. The railroad locomotive represented the highest form of technological development, and therefore was decorated in the most elaborate ways imaginable. *Jupiter* and No. 119 were typical, if exemplary, specimens of the glorious locomotives rolling the rails in 1869.

Author Jim Wilke, in his article titled "Victorian Splendor at Promontory" (*Locomotive & Railway Preservation* magazine, September/October 1994), describes *Jupiter* as "the mechanical equivalent of a brass band." Painted in brilliant colors, accented with ornate gold trim and shining brass accouterments,

Jupiter typified the passenger locomotive. Proud of their service, and looking to further their public image, the railroads spared no expense in decorating locomotives—particularly those used to haul passenger trains. Fueling the impetus for elegant decoration were some forty locomotive builders, all competing for new orders. Besides, the Victorian period favored elaborate decor, evidenced by its gingerbread architecture and colorful advertising posters.

Jupiter's wheels and cab trim flared a blazing crimson, while its cowcatcher, sand dome, cab, and tender were painted a brilliant blue with just a hint of violet. The boiler jacketing made of highly polished "Russian Iron" assumed a more subdued charcoal gray coloring, while the cylinders, steam dome, bell, and piping all gleamed with highly polished brass. Its name was proudly printed in small gold letters on its cab and large ones on its tender. Decorative striping covered all of its mechanical parts, and gold stars accented its wheel hubs. The smokestack, a typical balloon type, stood out for its lack of decoration—probably its propensity for sootiness made excessive design and color both unnecessary and undesirable.

The locomotive crews took extreme pride in their engines. Typically, each crew was assigned its own engine and was required to maintain it. Since firing up a steam locomotive would normally require several hours, plenty of time could be found to polish the bell, wipe down the drivers, and keep the locomotive looking sharp.

Jupiter was one of four identical locomotives delivered to Central Pacific in the spring of 1869; all were sent waiting final assembly via ship around Cape Horn, a more than four-month voyage. Jupiter was assigned the number 60, and its siblings were the *Storm*, No. 61; the *Whirlwind*, No. 62; and the *Leviathan*, No. 63. Luckily for Central Pacific, the most regal of the group was available for the Golden Spike ceremony.

Like most Central Pacific locomotives of the time, *Jupiter* burned wood for fuel. It had sixty-inch (152cm) driving wheels and could handle freight trains in addition to its usual passenger duties. Its normal speed would have been about thirty-five miles per hour (56 kph), though it could have traveled much faster on good track. *Jupiter* saw many years of service on the railroad following its appearance at Promontory, running the length of the line from Ogden, Utah, to Oakland, California. It is believed to have been scrapped soon after the turn of the century.

Union Pacific's No. 119 was certainly the less impressive ceremonial locomotive at Promontory on that crisp, clear, spring morning. But the locomotive was undoubtedly only a minor embarrassment to Union Pacific's Dr. Thomas C.

ABOVE: One of the most famous locomotives in the United States, *Jupiter* represented the railroad at the Golden Spike ceremony at Promontory, Utah, on May 10, 1869.

Durant, who was probably more concerned about his late arrival than trivialities of locomotive styling. The black-and-white photos do not do No. 119 justice, either. It is by no means the type of Spartan utilitarian machine that would serve railroads in years to come. In most respects it rivaled *Jupiter*'s styling, though certainly the latter machine possessed greater finesse. What is most amazing is that this common freight locomotive, one built to a standard pattern, featured such ornate decoration.

No. 119, and its four nearly identical siblings, had an elaborately decorated cab in the Italianate style popular at the time. The cab was constructed of wal-nut, and the decor of the locomotive embraced a walnut theme: walnuts could be found in several places on the engine. It featured lots of showy polished brass, but because we have no color photos of the original No. 119, and there do not appear to be detailed descriptions of its color (a luxury enjoyed by *Jupiter*), it is unknown precisely what colors No. 119 sported. However, it is quite probable that its wheels were painted red. Because it was intended for freight service, its primary colors were likely more subdued than those of *Jupiter*. However, like *Jupiter*, No. 119 featured elaborate scrolling, although not quite as detailed. One colorful feature found on No. 119, not found on its Central Pacific counterpart, were four unique oil paintings, each depicting an idyllic scene.

Since No. 119 featured an extended smoke box, intended to prevent sparks from exiting the stack, the engine was equipped with neither a balloon stack nor one of the diamond variety, often used on locomotives from that period to act as spark arresters. Instead it had a tall, straight smokestack. The Union Pacific had few trees along its route, therefore No. 119 burned coal for fuel instead of wood. Its cylinders were placed at a slight incline, indicative of an older design, though No. 119 was built in 1868, making it a relatively new locomotive at the time. The Civil War had caused a dramatic increase in the cost of new locomotives, and No. 119 cost roughly thirteen thousand dollars, more than twice the price of an equivalent locomotive before the war. Before it arrived at Promontory, No. 119 and its siblings spent much of their time with work trains building the Union Pacific. For that reason, perhaps, it was an appropriate, if serendipitous, choice for Union Pacific's representative at the railroads' joining. After more than thirty years of service, and at least one renumbering, this faithful locomotive was scrapped.

Today, operating replicas of both locomotives can be found at the Golden Spike National Historic Site. The ceremony is recreated every day in the summer for the benefit of admiring tourists.

PAGES 36–37: The Central Pacific's *Jupiter* was a typically colorful locomotive of the Victorian period.

ABOVE: *A view of the spike ceremony from the top of Union Pacific's No. 119. This ceremony was one of the best-documented events of the period.*

The Big Four of the Central Pacific had hoped for a meeting point much farther east—a goal largely foiled because of the extreme difficulties of construction in the High Sierra. Meanwhile, Union Pacific forces were hoping for a spot farther west. At different times each railroad jumped way ahead of its contiguous construction in an effort to take on more territory and gain more subsidy. The stakes were high and cooperation between the two railroads was low. One especially tense moment erupted when overlapping grading parties—one from each railroad—encountered each another in Utah's Echo Canyon. A skirmish resulted.

That issue, like many others that hampered the progress of the railroad, was resolved. The meeting point at Promontory was established, and for the moment, all differences were set aside in order to celebrate the railroad's completion.

Finally the tracks neared each other, and both railroads planned to show off their very best. The Spike Ceremony had been set for May 8, 1869, but it was not to be. Delays and natural disasters conspired against the celebrants. Despite good intentions, the plans were altered and the ceremony was postponed, finally occurring on May 10. Union Pacific's celebrity attendees, including the railroad's Vice President Durant, experienced a substantial delay when their special train was stopped and held for ransom by angry railroad workers demanding back wages. That crisis resolved, they were further delayed when heavy rains produced flash floods in eastern Utah. The raging water destroyed a new bridge deep in Echo Canyon near Devils Gate. This disaster was not easily overcome, and the fancy locomotive and ornate Pullmans destined for Promontory were left behind. A common train was commandeered to carry the Durant party the rest of the way to the ceremonial site.

The Central Pacific contingency also had its share of difficulties. Central Pacific's President Stanford and company's special train featured a dolled-up locomotive and exquisite Palace Cars. It experienced an unfortunate encounter with a fallen tree at Donner Pass. Less impressive—although elegant—transportation was arranged in the aftermath, and Stanford arrived at the set date, only to wait for his Union Pacific counterparts.

At long last, the parties were in place and the hastily planned event was to take place. The gala spike ceremony—documented by several photographers, including Matthew Brady's protégé A. J. Russell—has been shrouded in myth since that very day. We

short time, and under extremely harsh conditions: Sierra winters, Nevada summers, hostilities with Native Americans, and the tumultuous political and financial climate of the American Civil War. Yet, despite these hardships, the Pacific Railroad was completed, allowing through passage from East to West.

Promontory, Utah, a remote, windswept spot, barren save for some sage, is located to the north of that vast inland sea, the Great Salt Lake. Central Pacific built eastward from Sacramento (it is one of the few railroads in United States history built from west to east), while Union Pacific built westward from Omaha, Nebraska. Each railroad, anticipating this event, had raced across the West, laying tracks as fast as possible. At one frantic point Central Pacific track crews laid some ten miles (16km) of line in one working day, a long-standing record in the annals of railroad construction. Since the financial incentives offered by the United States government were based on each mile of completed line, the railroads were encouraged to build fast.

know it was a cold, clear afternoon. But the accounts of the event differ greatly on the details. Regardless, the essence of the event has become part of the American consciousness. Like much of popular history, the particulars are blurred for the sake of show.

To the railroads, the event was underwhelming, an anticlimax to the drama of building the railroad. Thousands of partisans were anticipated, but only some six hundred actually participated. Most notable was, of course, Central Pacific's flamboyant orator-politician Leland Stanford. But he was the only member of the

Big Four in attendance. Also present were Union Pacific's Dr. Thomas C. Durant; General Grenville Dodge, Union Pacific's chief engineer; and John "Jack" Casement, the man who was largely responsible for the direction of Union Pacific's construction. A potpourri of regional politicians, civic officials, and government representatives; a contingent of soldiers from the Twenty-first Infantry, including the Tenth Ward Headquarters Band; and a mix of railroad workers and wealthy sightseers rounded out the crowd of celebrants.

ABOVE: *The Central Pacific's illustrious president, Leland Stanford (center, holding up mallet), was the only member of the Big Four in attendance at the spike ceremony.*

RIGHT: *Locomotive No. 119 represented the Union Pacific at the Golden Spike ceremony at Promontory, Utah. The Union Pacific had intended to send a much fancier locomotive, but unanticipated events in the East precluded its participation.*

The two trains—the eastward-facing Central Pacific special led by *Jupiter* and the westward facing Union Pacific train led by locomotive No. 119—were brought to their respective "ends of track." Track gangs laid rails connecting the two railroads. Iron spikes were driven to secure the rails in place. When the last rails were in place, a prayer was given by the Reverend Dr. John Todd of Massachusetts and speeches were made proclaiming the great significance of the event.

At this point in the tale, accounts differ considerably. Many indicate that the final tie—a polished laurel specimen rather than one of the crude run-of-the-mill variety—was laid in place. A telegrapher stood by, key in hand, relaying the elements of the event to the world. Some say the final spike and mallet were wired, so that the final contact would relay an electrical signal to indicate the railroad's completion. Several commemorative spikes were placed; some silver, others gold. Leland Stanford was given the honor of placing the final gold spike—eighteen carats and nearly six inches (15cm) long bearing the words "The Last Spike." It is said Stanford gripped the ceremonial silver mallet, swung, and missed. Thomas Durant of Union Pacific was then given an opportunity, but he fared the same. Some say that the hilts of swords were used in lieu of heavy sledges. At 12:47 p.m., the telegrapher, disregarding trivialities of whether or not the spike had been struck, relayed the spirit of the action and transmitted the word "Done!"

This simple word eloquently and succinctly summed up the entire event. Celebration erupted around the nation. In thirty-seven states, various territories, and the nation's capital, cannons fired, bands played, and people marched and paraded. In New York City, the Wall Street stock exchange closed early.

Oblivious to celebrations elsewhere, other dignitaries finished what Stanford and Durant set out to do. No quicker than they were placed, the ceremonial spikes and tie were removed for safekeeping. The pilots of the locomotives were brought together, the band played, photographs were taken, and bottles of champagne were spilled liberally to mark the occasion. Soon spirits were flowing, and not just on the dry Utah soil!

With this event the world shrunk. What had previously taken months, now took only a few days.

But two thousand miles away, in the rolling hills of rural Massachusetts, a lonely widow celebrated another event. It was Anna Judah's wedding anniversary.

OPPOSITE: *Promontory, Utah, was the site of the joining of the Union Pacific and the Central Pacific. The site is often mistakenly called Promontory Point, a different location about thirty miles (48.3km) to the south, where the present-day Union Pacific now crosses the Great Salt Lake.*

EL GOBERNADOR

Leland Stanford wanted the world's largest locomotive for his Central Pacific—fitting for a man with sufficient ego to connect the rails of the nation's first transcontinental railroad. To accomplish the daunting task of producing such an animal, Stanford relied on Central Pacific's talented master mechanic, Andrew Jackson Stevens.

A. J. Stevens was an able man whose abilities as an inventor supplemented his mechanical skills. A native New Englander, he was hired by Stanford in 1867 to repair the company's locomotive fleet, then quickly promoted to master mechanic. Stevens was highly respected and well liked by his employees, and highly regarded at the Sacramento shops where he worked.

In 1872 and 1873 he pioneered locomotive building on the West Coast by beginning to design and construct locomotives at Sacramento. Before this, all new locomotives had to be purchased from Eastern builders. The railroad sought independence from Eastern builders—particularly Baldwin, with whom C. P. Huntington had an ongoing feud. This stemmed from the builder's insistence on cash payment for locomotives during the railroad's tenuous formative period. While Central Pacific continued to purchase some locomotives from the East, it successfully manufactured many of its own locomotives for many years.

The standard locomotive through much of the nineteenth century was the American type, with its 4-4-0 wheel arrangement (two pairs of guiding wheels, followed by two pairs of driving wheels and no wheels trailing). Henry Campbell, a civil engineer for the Philadelphia & Germantown railroad, first conceived of the 4-4-0 in 1836. This type of engine quickly gained pop-

ularity because of its easy treatment of track and universal service adaptability. By the turn of the century nearly twenty-five thousand 4-4-0s had been built. It is only natural that Stevens' first locomotive would be of this type. When completed, it was fifty-two feet (16m) long and weighed sixty-six thousand pounds (29,964kg)—comparable to other locomotives of its type. This was the first of more than seventy locomotives built at Sacramento during Stevens' tenure, but not by any means the most famous.

By the early 1880s the volume of traffic moving over the Sierra on the transcontinental route had grown substantially. The railroad was looking for more powerful locomotives to hoist its trains over the 2.4-percent ruling westbound grade up to the summit at Donner Pass. This climb, with more than ninety miles (145km) of grade and its many miles of snowsheds, was one of the most formidable mountain crossings in the West. While the 4-4-0 was fine for passenger trains, local freight service, or even heavier runs in level territory, such as California's Central Valley, it was not preferred for service up on "the mountain." From the beginning, Central Pacific used ten wheelers, featuring a 4-6-0 wheel arrangement for heavy freight service in the Sierra. The first Central Pacific ten wheeler was an 1865 product of William Mason in Taunton, Massachusetts, named *Coness*. It was fifty-two feet (16m) long, weighed nearly 120,000 pounds (54,480kg) and featured forty-eight-inch (122cm) driving wheels. These locomotives had proved effective, but the railroad wanted greater pulling power, so in 1881 Central Pacific encouraged Stevens to build a larger, more powerful locomotive. The Lehigh Valley railroad had experimented with a 4-8-0 locomotive called a Mastodon type, so Stevens decided to design and build one as well. In 1882 he completed the railroad's first 4-8-0, numbered

229. This locomotive, largely the original design of Stevens and his associates, proved very successful. It could do the work of three older ten wheelers hauling heavy freight trains over Donner Pass. The railroad was pleased and sent the locomotive to a railroad exposition in Chicago, where it awed viewers. An order for twenty-five similar locomotives was placed with the Cooke Locomotive Works of Paterson, New Jersey.

At this juncture, Central Pacific president Leland Stanford pushed Stevens a step further, asking him to build the largest locomotive in the world. Obeying Stanford's wishes, Stevens began designing an unprecedented 4-10-0. The story of this monstrous locomotive nearly came to an end when the railroad's vice president, another one of the Big Four, Charlie Crocker, discovered the locomotive's frame under construction at the Sacramento shops. A practical man, Crocker viewed the project as a waste of company resources and ordered it stopped. He was soon overruled by Stanford—who was not to be denied the world's largest locomotive because of practicality—and the locomotive was completed. In 1883 Stevens' 4-10-0, named *El Gobernador*, was unveiled. An impressive beast, the enormous locomotive was truly the world's largest. While *El Gobernador* resembled Stevens' *Mastodon* in much of its outward appearance—including the distinctive clerestory cab—its appearance differed in one very significant respect: where the *Mastodon* had four sets of drivers, *El Gobernador* featured five pairs of fifty-seven-inch (145 centimeter) wheels and weighed a tremendous 154,000 pounds (69,916kg).

Unfortunately, *El Gobernador* 's only redeeming features were its superlative dimensions: the locomotive did not run well; its firebox did not allow for sufficient steam to haul heavy trains in the Sierra. After a year or so it was disassembled and transferred in pieces (the railroad feared it would be too heavy to run over the bridges in the Central Valley) to Bakersfield, California, for use in helper service in the Tehachapis.

Then recently completed, the line to Los Angeles through the Tehachapi Mountains below Bakersfield was the work of William Hood, an engineering genius who worked on many of the Big Four's Central Pacific and Southern

Pacific grades. The steeply graded, sinuous Tehachapi crossing was characteristic of Hood's style of construction: tracks gained elevation and maintained a steady grade by following the natural lines of the land and required only a minimal amount of earth moving and bridge building. Yet despite this minimalism, the rugged nature of the Tehachapis required more than a dozen tunnels and featured one of Hood's most recognized landmarks, the world-famous Tehachapi Loop. Winding along Caliente Creek, the track loops up and over itself to maintain a steady climb to the 3,969-foot (1,210m) Tehachapi Summit. Traversing the grassy, rolling California hills, accented by occasional oaks and patches of wildflowers, Southern Pacific's Tehachapi crossing remains one of the most photogenic railroad lines in the West, possibly the world.

Despite *El Gobernador* 's unsatisfactory performance in the Sierra, the locomotive found steady work climbing the grade between Bakersfield and the Mojave Desert. It was restricted primarily to mainline operation—the railroad was concerned about the effects of its weight on passing sidings. The Tehachapi route is primarily composed of single track with sidings at strategic locations to allow trains to pass. The exceptional locomotive was unpopular with railroad crews because of its limitations, lack of power, and propensity to run low on water. In 1893 the railroad sent it back to Sacramento ostensibly for rebuilding, however it never ran again and was eventually dismantled. It remains the only 4-10-0 ever built for an American railroad, and also the last Central Pacific locomotive to receive a name in addition to a number.

OPPOSITE: Andrew Jackson Stevens, Central Pacific's first master mechanic. ABOVE: One of Stevens' Mastodon-type locomotives. PAGES 46–47: Based on A. J. Stevens' successful 4-8-0 Mastodon-type locomotive, *El Gobernador* was the largest locomotive in the world when it was built, and the only 4-10-0 type ever to roll on American rails. Although very large, the locomotive was not very successful, and it spent much of its time in the shop.

CHAPTER TWO

TRAINS ACROSS THE PLAINS

OPPOSITE: *A Santa Fe train crew poses with their locomotive in front of the depot at Pratt, Kansas. Traditionally, train crews were composed of a locomotive engineer, fireman, conductor, and at least a couple of brakemen.*

RAILS ALONG THE SANTA FE TRAIL

In the 1850s, a Pennsylvania visionary named Cyrus Holliday dreamed of a railroad that would extend across the plains to the distant Spanish trading post of Santa Fe. This shining iron road would follow the old Santa Fe Trail and carry the goods of old Mexico to the East in fine railroad style. Like Theodore Judah, Holliday was a dreamer—and also a determined one.

Santa Fe, located in the southwestern desert, was one of the oldest established Western settlements in North America, dating back to the early seventeenth century. In the early 1820s, before the first commercial railroad turned a wheel in North America, Santa Fe had become a principal trading post for Mexicans, Native Americans, and traders from the United States. The legendary Santa Fe Trail was a loosely defined rutted path running westward across the plains from Independence, Missouri, to Santa Fe, and was used for some sixty years by ox-drawn wagons. Following the Mexican War in 1846, Santa Fe and the surrounding territory became part of the United States. Not long afterward, a young Cyrus Holliday began to envision a railroad to serve Santa Fe and the Kansas plains.

Holliday had to rely upon his wits, labor, and ability to convince his comrades of the benefits of his idea. And after years of planning, scheming, lobbying, and sweat, Holliday finally watched as the first train of the Atchison, Topeka & Santa Fe rolled out across the plains, hauled by the locomotive named in honor of Mr. Holliday. It was a short trip, just seven miles (11km) from Topeka to Cottonwood Grove, Kansas, but it was the first step in what would become one of the greatest railroads in the West. Mr. Holliday made a prophetic speech at Cottonwood Grove, explaining how some day the railroad would stretch to many places far and wide, including San Francisco and Mexico City. Just a few weeks later, Leland Stanford of the Central Pacific would seal the gap between his road and the Union Pacific at Promontory. But to Cyrus Holliday, it was the slow and sure progress of the Santa Fe that mattered. This line was his road.

The early days of the Santa Fe were rife with logistical problems. Financial concerns aside, it was a difficult line to build and operate. In the 1870s, Kansas was wild territory, and its vast wide-open plains presented a variety of challenges to the Santa Fe employees. Hostile Native Americans were a threat to the railroad, as they had been to earlier wagon trains, but lawless cowboys and bandits often proved a greater concern. Nature took its toll, too: stampeding herds of wild buffalo; fierce, blinding snow storms, dust storms, and tornadoes; and plagues of grasshoppers.

Early on, Santa Fe's rails reached untamed Newton, Kansas, a town noted for its desperadoes and dangerous lifestyle. Railroad employees, generally regarded as more civilized than the common cowhand, occasionally became entangled in the lawless adventures that made the Old West famous. One such adventure began in a Newton saloon in August 1871. A Santa Fe employee, known as Mike McCluskie, found himself in an irreconcilable argument with a boorish rake from Texas named Ed Baylor. McCluskie was already a Santa Fe veteran, and he often wore a "Thousand Mile shirt," a prize given to employees with that many miles of service. This trophy apparently did not impress Mr. Baylor, who after a time, unable to tolerate the railroader's attitude, drew his gun to shoot him. Evidently McCluskie anticipated Baylor's action, and before the Texan could pull the trigger, McCluskie shot Baylor instead.

Back then, justice in Newton was delivered by whomever drew first, and a dead man's appeal might come from his friend's six-shooter, as Santa Fe's McCluskie soon found out. Old Baylor had not wandered up from the Lone Star State alone. He had come with a gang of friends who were now distraught over his untimely end. They tracked down McCluskie at a local dancehall where they returned the favor he had done Baylor. But the bloodshed did not stop there. Mike McCluskie had a Good Samaritan streak in him, and through his deeds he had earned a friend who

LEFT: *To promote the railroads, their owners often staged first- and last-spike ceremonies to drum up public support and encourage investors.*

would not tolerate his passing. In McCluskie's travels, he had rescued a poor, sick boy named Dennis Riley riding westward aboard a Zulu—the nickname for a poorly equipped immigrant car. Riley repaid McCluskie's kindness by dispatching Baylor's avengers with a hail of angry bullets. Soon afterward, Riley vanished in the great expanse of the West and was never again seen in Newton.

Trigger fingers were pretty sensitive in those days, so much so that many Santa Fe engineers opted to turn their headlights off when running at night through particularly unruly towns. The mere sight of a faintly glowing kerosene light could easily attract the guns of drunken cowboys. Evidently it was considered safer to risk hitting a stray cow than to risk getting gratuitously shot.

Stray cattle did prove a problem from time to time. Since the early days of the West, cattle had roamed free, and this, along with stampeding buffalo, caused a variety of difficulties. More often than not a train would be merely delayed, as the fireman jumped down from the locomotive and attempted to shoo clumsy bovines off the tracks. Since cattle often traveled in large numbers, this could result in substantive delays on the open plain. Occasionally, though, a lonely cow wandered helplessly into the path of a train. The worst wreck on the line in 1870 occurred when train No. 4 backed into a stray cow, causing twenty-five dollars worth of damage to the train, and totaling the cow!

In 1873, in Illinois, a man named Joseph Glidden invented something that would soon make encounters with stray cattle a less frequent occurrence. This simple but effective invention forever changed the raising of livestock in the West. Mr. Glidden's invention is the now ubiquitous barbed wire. Barbed wire and railroads quickly transformed the wide-open prairies into productive agricultural land. As ranchers and farmers settled in, the wild days of cattle drives came to an end.

Soon the plains of Kansas were as safe as any place back East. Eventually, Santa Fe engineers could securely run with their headlights on at night without fear of sudden, unplanned, lead-induced ventilation. And, while the Santa Fe never reached Mexico City, it did reach most of the places that Cyrus Holliday envisioned, spanning much of the Southwest from Chicago to San Francisco, with lines to Texas and Los Angeles.

FRED HARVEY

The early days of Western railroad travel were not known for culinary delights. On the contrary, the primitive, rudimentary railroad eateries left a legacy of indigestion, heartburn, and food poisoning. Before the dining car was adopted as a standard accouterment to long-distance trains, passengers had to disembark at trackside beaneries to eat. A fully loaded train would pull up and unload the entirety of its passengers, who then had ten or fifteen minutes to order and eat. The quality of the food was abysmal, the service was worse, and virtually no time was allotted to consume meals. The entire experience was rushed, crowded, and, on the whole, unpleasant.

On the Santa Fe, a British-born gentleman named Fred Harvey changed that sorry situation. Mr. Harvey had fine tastes and was simply appalled by the pal-

try eating accommodations on the Western railroads. So he combined his two skills, railroading and restauranting, and offered what he believed was necessary to improve the standards of civilized travel: quality dining. Fred Harvey first proposed his idea to the Chicago, Burlington, & Quincy—colloquially known simply as the "Q"—which, not so coincidentally, was also his employer at the time. But when the Q dismissed his idea, Harvey went to the Santa Fe. Charles F. Morse, Santa Fe's superintendent, endorsed Harvey's quality-dining concept, and in 1876 Fred Harvey assumed the food-service operation at Topeka, Kansas.

Harvey immediately improved service at the station restaurant. He established a standard rate for meals—at that time fifty cents—offered a variety of tasty dishes, provided ample portions, and most important, did not rush his

ABOVE: Fred Harvey founded one of America's first successful restaurant chains. OPPOSITE: Before Harvey Houses, dining aboard the Western rails was abysmal. Entire trainloads of passengers were given ten or fifteen minutes to disembark, get a meal, and reboard.

patrons. His formula was an instant success and soon the Santa Fe awarded him more business. Yet Harvey did not just up and quit his job with the Q; he had a wife and five children to feed, and it was only after his restaurants were firmly established that he devoted his full attention to food service. Once he did, the business really flourished. Within a few years he was operating dozens of restaurants and hotels along the Santa Fe. And, as the Santa Fe expanded to new horizons, so did Fred Harvey. He was a man of honor and principle; he preferred the handshake to the written contract, and for years he did business with Santa Fe without any formal paperwork.

His name was associated with one of America's first successful chain restaurants, known universally as "Harvey Houses." From Chicago to Los Angeles, all across the plains, and Southwest along the mighty Santa Fe, the Harvey House was an institution of quality and civility. Some of his best-known establishments were the Harvey Houses at Barstow, California; Holbrook, Arizona; and the Casteñada hotel and restaurant at Las Vegas, New Mexico. Fred Harvey was known for high quality; he paid top dollar for his supplies and always demanded the very best. He did not blink at having to pay $1.50 for a dozen prairie chickens or ten cents for a pound of butter. He paid his employees equally well. At one point he hired a chef at an annual salary of five thousand dollars to work in one of his restaurants. This was unprecedented—most railroad workers were happy to earn two dollars a day!

By 1888 he had raised the price of his meals to seventy-five cents and his menu included some of the best and most exotic food offered by any American railroad. At one restaurant the menu listed Lobster Salad au Mayonnaise, Pickled Lamb's Tongue, Young Capon in Hollandaise Sauce, Baked Veal Pie, English Peas au Gratin, Salmi of Duck, Charlotte of Peaches, Cold Custard à la Chantilly, bananas, and more traditional items such as stuffed turkey, roast beef sirloin, and apple pie. This was a dramatic improvement over the beans and fried beefsteak available at other railroad restaurants. It's no wonder the traveling public preferred the Santa Fe over "them other railroads." However, Fred Harvey's impeccable standards did not apply just to his food. His help, too, was of the finest quality, and probably did more than any other feature of his restaurants to promote his reputation. To serve his patrons, he hired only civilized, intelligent, attractive, and well-behaved young ladies. They were known as the "Harvey Girls."

As with many of the items on the menu, Harvey had to import his help. In the old West there was a noticeable deficiency of the type of women Harvey wished to employ, so he looked to the East, particularly New England, for his

Harvey Girls. He offered secure employment and high wages, but in return asked that the women remain unmarried for at least one year. From the number of quick marriages that took place it would appear that Fred Harvey did not strictly enforce this policy. Many a Santa Fe engineer, conductor, trainman, and yard clerk who went into one of Harvey's many fine establishments found more than his morning vittles! One preposterous estimate credits more than four thousand babies being named in honor of Mr. Harvey. The point is well made—he brought about a great many weddings in the West.

Harvey Girls were paid $17.50 a month, and lived in rent-free dormitories chaperoned by a matron. The girls were required to be in bed by ten o'clock, and were expected to uphold high moral standards. This sort of practice was not unique to the highly principled Harvey. Remember that in the 1850s C. P. Huntington expected similar behavior from his male employees.

Harvey's high standards were applied to his patrons, too. He expected all men eating at his restaurants to be dressed appropriately. For those who did not have proper attire, Harvey would provide alpaca coats. Those who chose not to wear a dinner coat were not served. In the days of the Western frontier, this policy cause Harvey some difficulties.

Every so often some uncivilized customers lacking the required attire would wander into a Harvey establishment and demand service. Rowdy behavior was not tolerated, and boors, louts, and other troublemakers were encouraged to follow the same standards as other patrons. More than once, gun-toting cowboys rode into a Harvey House, made a scene, demanded service, and let loose a few bullets to make their point known. On one of these occasions, in 1882, Mr. Harvey, who happened to be having dinner, coolly confronted the pistol-toting desperadoes and shamed them into behaving in a proper, genteel fashion. He also fed them free

of charge. No one was hurt, and the subdued cowboys enjoyed a free meal in proper attire.

In Oklahoma, Harvey's coat policy was challenged in court. The state's corporate commissioner was outraged when he was denied his meal for failing to don proper Harvey attire and sued on the grounds that coat wearing was contrary to Sooner custom. Harvey won the case; the judge felt that Harvey's civilizing was a welcome action in an otherwise uncivilized territory.

In 1893 Fred Harvey's business took on a new dimension as he began operating Santa Fe's dining cars. The rolling restaurant soon took the place of a

A "LIMITED EXPRESS."
"Five seconds for Refreshments"!

number of wayside Harvey houses, although many of Harvey's restaurants continued to operate for years.

Fred Harvey died in 1901, but his legacy of quality, good service, and pretty waitresses lived on for many years. In 1945 Judy Garland forever immortalized the Harvey Girl in the American imagination when she starred in the Metro-Goldwyn-Mayer movie *The Harvey Girls*.

THE <u>OVERLAND</u> LIMITED

Few trains had the name recognition of the *Overland Limited*. Tying the East and the West together, the *Overland Limited* offered reliable, fast, and safe transportation between Chicago and San Francisco for decades. Luxurious accommodations, consistently good service, and modern amenities gave the *Overland* a reputation as one of the best trains in the West. For many travelers, the *Overland* was simply the only way west. Other routes and other trains simply would not do.

The *Overland Limited* carried more than its share of famous persons, from politicians and presidents to financiers, actors, playboys, and foreign dignitaries. The great populist orator and presidential hopeful William Jennings Bryan, whose several attempts at attaining the high office all ended in failure, was an *Overland* passenger. More successful candidates, such as William McKinley, Theodore Roosevelt, and William H. Taft, all rode to San Francisco (Oakland, really) aboard *Overland* luxury Pullman Palace cars. The great financier J. P. Morgan, who in his day controlled billions of investment dollars and who was considered by many to be the most powerful man in the world, regularly rode the Union Pacific's finest in his travels. So, too, did Gen. John J. Pershing, Prince Albert of Belgium, and England's Duke of Manchester.

Union Pacific introduced the *Overland Flyer* in 1887 as a first-class "transcontinental run." It grew in stature upon the premature discontinuation of the *Golden Gate Special* in 1889, and in 1896 Union Pacific renamed the train the *Overland Limited*. Southern Pacific, which had been forwarding the train over its Central Pacific route in conjunction with Union Pacific since its beginning, recognized the *Overland* name in 1899. This premier service was reflected in the *Overland*'s scheduled numbers: the westbound *Overland* operated as No. 1, and the eastbound as No. 2. East of Omaha, Chicago & Northwestern and Milwaukee Road variously forwarded the train to Chicago.

Speed and comfort were hallmarks of the *Overland*. In 1899 Union Pacific touted the train as the fastest and most luxurious. And it was indeed swift, making the long run between Chicago and San Francisco in just seventy-three hours! Comfort was

RIGHT: *The* Overland Limited *observation car was designed for luxurious enjoyment of Western scenery. It accommodated passengers with plush comfortable chairs, large windows for clear views of passing vistas, and an open platform to enjoy clear Western skies.*

paramount in the finest Pullman Palace cars. Although it might not have been as richly opulent as the short-lived *Golden Gate Special*, the *Overland Limited* exuded quality and luxury. No high-minded traveler ever complained of shoddy or second-rate service aboard this train.

Union Pacific never rested with its premier service, and in 1902 it spent two million dollars to refurbish the train with the latest equipment. New wooden cars featured steel frames, the latest technological innovation and a vast improvement over earlier designs. Also added to the trains was a novel means of communication: the telephone.

A new force in railroading took control of the Union Pacific in the 1890s and the Southern Pacific following the turn of the century: New York financier E. H. Harriman, a man with ambition, insight, and resources to back up his plans. Under his progressive control both railroads benefited greatly. Harriman

implemented many improvements to the railroad's physical plant, ushering in a new era of speed, safety, and prosperity on the Union Pacific and Southern Pacific. On the Southern Pacific's old Central Pacific line, he built a vast causeway across the Great Salt Lake, bypassing Promontory and shortening the railroad's mileage. He started an ambitious plan to add a second mainline track over Donner Pass in the California Sierra. On the Union Pacific, he improved the railroad's right-of-way and physical plant to bring the railroad up to first-class standards.

Harriman was a safety nut. He equipped hundreds of miles of railroad with automatic block signals. By using an electric track circuit to indicate train occupancy, these signals greatly reduced the chance of rear-end collisions and other types of accidents. The Union Switch & Signal lower-quadrant semaphore—the predominant type of signal found on Harriman's railroads—became a symbol of safety, and images of the red-

LEFT: *The* Overland Limited *was the deluxe mode of travel to the West Coast, and it afforded passengers every comfort available, including such novelties as electric lighting.* **BELOW**: *This primitive manual block semaphore was a precursor to later automatic block signals that greatly improved railroad operations by allowing trains to operate faster and more safely. One of Harriman's many improvements to his railroads was the adoption of automatic block signals.*

and-yellow semaphore blades could be found throughout railroad literature for many years. But the signals were more than just safety devices. Automatic signaling had several additional benefits. It allowed trains to operate faster and more frequently without a significant increase in physical plant, thereby greatly increasing the railroad's capacity. Harriman's pioneering use of signaling set a trend in Western railroading. More than ninety years after some lower-quadrant semaphores were installed, they were still performing the job for which they were intended. A testimony to solid technology and a sound investment!

Plant improvements, additions of second mainline tracks, and automatic block signals all allowed for faster train schedules. Nowhere was this better reflected than in the *Overland Limited*'s tight timekeeping. The thirty miles of trestles across the Great Salt Lake were a significant improvement over the original line through Promontory. Instead of having to wind around the lake,

trains now zipped across it. The *Overland* at sea was an irresistible concept to the train's promoters, who posed the *Overland* on the Salt Lake trestles for publicity photographs.

With these improvements the schedule had been dramatically improved: seventy-three hours' running time fell to seventy. As hours were cut from its running time, the train was advertised with a proud eagle soaring over its semaphore-protected consist.

San Francisco Overland Limited

    Extra Fare

    Finest and Fastest

    Only 63-hour Train Between Chicago and

    San Francisco

Glowing prose was unnecessary when advertising the *Overland*; the simple facts told the story.

THE LIGHTNING EXPRESS

In the United States' centennial year, 1876, an air of popular excitement often led to wild publicity stunts. The Pacific Railroad was still a darling of transportation in the eyes of the public; only seven years had passed since the Golden Spike ceremony at Promontory. What could be better than testing the limits of this new resource? The Pacific Railroad had cut transit time between New York and California from weeks to days. But just how quickly could the transcontinental run be made? Two theater producers wanted to find out.

Henry Jarrett and Lawrence Palmer, owners of a theatrical production of Shakespeare's *Henry V*, wished to close their New York production on a Wednesday evening and whisk their entire production team to San Francisco in just four days for a grand opening the following Monday. To do so would require unprecedented overland speed. According to the normal running times on the railroads involved, the trip would take at least a week. To accomplish this goal, Jarrett and Palmer chartered a special train, making exclusive arrangements with the railroads to haul it nonstop from coast to coast. They did so in style, with all the pomp and circumstance of the era. A three-car train was assembled consisting of a coach, a baggage car, and the deluxe Pullman Hotel Car *Marlborough*.

Shortly after midnight on June 1, Lawrence Barrett—an American actor of Irish descent well known for his Shakespearean performances—and his supporting cast departed New York City. A ferry ride across the Hudson River brought them to their *Lightning Express*, which left from the large terminal in Jersey City and raced at record-breaking speeds across the nation. Not one to miss a grand promotional opportunity, the *New York Herald* got in on the action. From the train's baggage car, fresh copies of the newspaper were distributed liberally to cheering people along the route as the train zipped passed. All along the way efforts were made to keep the railroad clear of traffic, and the *Lightning Express* was given highest priority. While the train ran through, it was still necessary to change engines, and this was done as swiftly as possible. The Union Pacific assigned eight of its fastest locomotives to move the train across the great expanse of Nebraska, Wyoming, and Utah. The Central Pacific took the train at Ogden and sprinted across the Nevada deserts and over the High Sierra. To lead the special, Central Pacific polished up one of its finest: a proud, shiny, high-drivered (large wheels for speed), American-type 4-4-0. A product of Schenectady Works, No. 149, the *Black Fox*, was one of Central Pacific's five *Fox* locomotives. Experienced engineers Hank Small and James Wright were among the privileged crewmen who operated the fast train. In only two places were helpers (extra locomotives needed on especially steep sections

of line) added: over Donner Pass and over Altamont Pass, west of Tracy, California. The rest of the way the train operated unassisted.

The *Lightning Express* arrived in Oakland on June 4 in record time and the actors were ferried across the bay to San Francisco, where it is reported they feasted at the Palace Hotel. *Henry V* opened as scheduled at McCullough's California Theater. Accounts differ as to the train's running time. There was no standardized time in those days, and each locality had its own "sun time" (so-called "Standard Time" would come a decade later). One photo of the train by established San Francisco photographers Bradley and Rulofson indicates the running time as eighty-three hours, fifty-three minutes, and forty-five seconds. How could such a precise measurement be wrong? Another photo marking the event, taken by a different photographer, gives the time as eighty-three hours, fifty-nine minutes, and sixteen seconds. Other accounts reveal the time between Jersey City and San Francisco to be eighty-four hours and seventeen minutes,

including the boat ride across San Francisco Bay. In any case, the time was indeed less than half that normally scheduled for such a run. Pioneering "Forty-niners" living in San Francisco at the time must have marveled at the sheer wonder of crossing the continent at such speed. Many of them had spent months crossing the land on foot or sailing around the Horn. So who's to argue about a few minutes?

OPPOSITE: The Central Pacific used its handsome *Black Fox* loco-motive No. 149 to haul the *Lightning Express* on the final leg of its run. ABOVE: The *Lightning Express* was a one-time publicity stunt, running from coast to coast in record time—approximately eighty-four hours. Ten years earlier, before the completion of the railroad, the trip from coast to coast had been measured in weeks, rather than hours.

The Streamliner — "CITY OF SAN FRANCISCO" "GOING-TO-SEA-BY-RAIL".... CROSSING GREAT SALT LAKE, UTAH

By the 1920s, the schedule was cut to just fifty-eight hours between Chicago and San Francisco, and by 1930 another two hours were cut from the running time, giving the train a fifty-six-hour run. Impressive in the days before air travel!

Though speed was a primary concern to advertisers, and presumably to the traveling public, in most brochures the quality of the ride was stressed before the train's tight schedules. The *Overland* was the train of the discriminating passenger. When the railroad said "finest," they meant it. As the train whisked through the wide-open Western landscape, its passengers were enticed to enjoy a leisurely, carefree trip. This was not some cramped, uncomfortable passage of necessity, but a train of luxury. Certainly today's airlines could take a hint or two from the travel promotions of ninety years ago. In 1906 a pamphlet touting the *Overland Limited* described the train's splendid accommodations and the experience that passengers could anticipate:

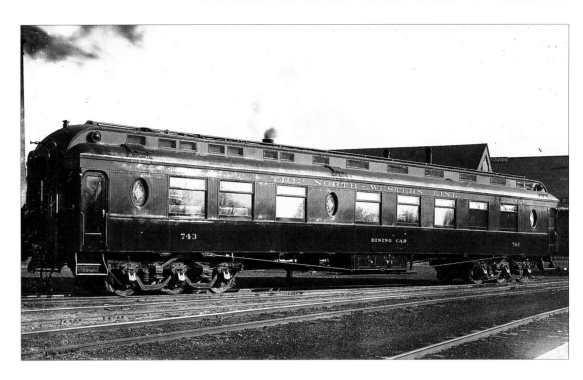

> *The trip contains no dull moments. Much time is spent in the composite car, where from the observation parlor, or from comfortable campchairs in the broad recesses of the brass-railed, rubber-tiled observation platform, the great panorama of the West is watched as it unfolds in fast-receding miles.*
>
> *At evening the ladies read and chat, the children play, the older members of the company sink comfortably into the big armchairs of the library, and the men gather in the smoking room, a delightful group in which tourists from all nations, army officers, and diplomats, men of affairs and their families, forget the outside world in the comradeship of travel.*
>
> *Social life on the Overland Limited during this journey of 70 hours is not unlike that on an ocean steamer, where a congenial company finds rest and recreation amid surroundings that include all the luxuries of twentieth century travel.*

One of the indulgences of turn-of-the-century first-class train travel was the dining car, and the *Overland* did not disappoint. Its dining cars were everything a discerning traveler had come to expect. One diner, the *Manhattan*, was a steel-framed, wooden affair, built by Pullman in 1900. It featured fully enclosed vestibules, one of the latest improvements in passenger-car design, which enabled passengers to pass between cars without being exposed to the elements. Like other cars on the *Overland*, it was illuminated by electric lights and was, in the restrained wording of Union Pacific, "As perfect [as] every accessory to elegance can make it."

In 1906 the *Overland*'s menu featured Essence of Beef, en Tasse; Chicken Okra, Southern Style; Pompano, Orléanaise; and Patties of Lake Shrimp, Newburg. The menu aboard the train was often changed so that regular patrons would not tire from monotonous eating. Just before the onset of the First World War, the menu in the diner offered *Overland* passengers a variety of delectable cuisine. From the exotic to the common, it was all very good. For the traditional patron, menu choices included Roast Young Turkey with Cranberries, sixty-five cents; Ribs of Prime Western Beef, sixty cents; Boiled Potatoes, ten cents; Mashed Potatoes, fifteen cents; Candied Sweet Potatoes, twenty cents. For those preferring something in the way of game, there was either Broiled Philadelphia Squab or Broiled Teal Duck for sixty-five cents. Those feeling more indulgent could order Roast Mallard Duck for $1.25. From the ocean, lakes, and streams there were plenty of choices for both appetizers and entrées: Canapé of Anchovies, twenty-five cents; Clear Green Turtle Soup, twenty-five cents; and Mountain Trout, Meunière, for sixty-five cents. There were also plenty of choices for dessert, including English Plum Pudding, for twenty-five cents; Hot Mince Pie with Brandy Sauce, for fifteen cents; and Ice Cream, for fifteen cents. There were a variety of teas for ten cents a pot, and coffee for fifteen cents a pot.

ABOVE: *Wooden dining cars like this were typically used on the Overland route. After the turn of the century, wooden car construction gave way to all steel construction primarily due to safety concerns—in wrecks, wooden cars would splinter and burn easily.*

OPPOSITE: *Under Harriman, the Southern Pacific built a new line, called the Lucin Cutoff, that greatly shortened the route between Ogden, Utah, and California by crossing the Salt Lake on a series of long trestles instead of going around it.*

THE <u>GOLDEN GATE SPECIAL</u>

Five days after the festivities at Promontory, Union Pacific and Central Pacific introduced through transcontinental passenger service on their Overland route between Omaha, Nebraska, and Sacramento, California. The trains on the route were given the distinctive numbers "1" and "2" on Central Pacific and "3" and "4" on Union Pacific. However, the trains' name, *Express*, suffered from a lack of imagination. Six months after its introduction, the service was extended all the way to Oakland, California. After a few years, the railroads named the westbound train the *Pacific Express* and the eastbound was called the *Atlantic Express*—despite the fact that the closest it came to the Atlantic Ocean was the Missouri River!

In the 1870s, the Overland route was the only show in town, providing the fastest, easiest method of transportation to the West Coast. Sleeping-car service was offered by Pullman on Union Pacific and by Jackson and Sharp on Central Pacific. The original service took five days and seven hours between end points, a vast improvement over the weeks and months of earlier nonrail routes. Also, the chances of contracting a tropical fever dropped precipitously.

By the mid-1880s, there were other ways of getting to the coast. The Northern Pacific and Santa Fe also offered rail routes to travelers. But while the Overland route had lost its strict monopoly on efficient West Coast travel, it still provided the only serious way of reaching San Francisco—then the only place on the West Coast of any real consequence. Competitive concerns aside, the Union Pacific wished to introduce a supreme deluxe service similar to those becoming popular on the East Coast. Not just a first-class train, but a train of exemplary quality and distinctive taste. On December 5, 1888, nearly twenty years after the Golden Spike, it introduced truly luxurious travel accommodations to the Bay Area from the Midwest: the *Golden Gate Special*. Fifty years before the famous suspension bridge would span the Golden Gate, the train bearing that name became for a short time a household word, equated with the utmost traveling splendor. Union Pacific spared no expense on the train or its advertising. In fact, Union Pacific carried out one of the greatest advertising campaigns of the time. Railroad schedules and brochures boldly promoted the *Golden Gate Special* as "The Finest Train in the World." Of the accuracy of this claim there is little doubt. It was among the most luxurious trains ever to roll on American rails. And the beautiful, ornate brochures did their best, with

colorful prose and detailed line drawings, to convey the majesty and elegance of this fantastic railroad extravagance.

The train operated on an expedited schedule in each direction once a week. Eastbound, it departed San Francisco at 2:00 p.m. and arrived in Council Bluffs, Iowa, three and a half days later. Westbound, it departed Council Bluffs at 8:00 a.m. for San Francisco and made the 1,867-mile (3,004km) run in similar time. A single consist of five specially equipped Pullmans provided the service. Since the train was entirely reserved and only carried long-distance passengers, it had no coaches. The baggage car was named *Golden Gate* and was always placed immediately behind the locomotive. In addition to storage for trunks and other heavy baggage, this car featured a barber shop and men's bathroom. The dining car, where travelers could anticipate only the finest meals, was the *Casa Monica*. Two elegantly decorated twelve-section sleeping cars, named *Khiva* and *Rahula*, featured rich carpeting, beautifully designed drapery and upholstery, and highly polished mahogany. The observation-sleeper, *Aladdin*, always brought up the rear of the train. It was one of the very first rear-end observation cars and featured large plate-glass windows and an open platform with polished brass railing for viewing Western splendor. Inside, it contained six

sleeping compartments, a buffet and drawing room, and a library. One of the most marvelous features of the *Special* was its electric lamps—ornate decorative chandeliers, in the spirit of the luxurious detailed decor. Indeed, passengers may have felt they were rivaling Jules Verne's fabulous excursion, *Around the World in Eighty Days*.

The *Special* catered exclusively to the needs of the rich and influential, and surely must have carried some of the most influential and respected people of the time. It was priced accordingly: the one-way fare was one hundred dollars per person, a tremendous amount of money in the days when many earned only a dollar a day. A ride in a sleeper aboard the *Golden Gate Special* might even cost highly paid railroad engineers more than a month's wages. Other first-class trains to the coast only charged one tenth that fare. Furthermore, services aboard the train were not included with the fare. The on-board barber would charge seventy-five cents for a shave and a haircut, not including gratuity.

There are no known photographs of the *Special* on the road, although there are nice line drawings and images of the passenger equipment. It is unknown precisely what sort of locomotives were used on the train, although it is very likely well-dressed, American-type 4-4-0s had the honor. About the same time as the *Special's* inauguration, Union Pacific experimented with fast, high-drivered Americans in a center-cab, or "Mother Hubbard," configuration. This type of locomotive enjoyed considerable popularity on the anthracite-hauling coal railroads in the East—particularly Pennsylvania—but never saw much use in the West. The engineer rode up on top of the boiler in a special cab that straddled the engine, while the fireman rode behind. It's not difficult to believe that Union Pacific used these special locomotives on their fastest train, although we have no record to show it.

While the concept was sound and its execution impeccable, the train itself was a failure. After only six months it was discontinued without explanation. Its cars were reassigned to other duties, and passengers were diverted to other runs, notably the *Overland Flyer*. Perhaps the high cost of riding the *Special* discouraged even the most wealthy of its potential patrons. And certainly a more-frequent schedule might have attracted more patrons. Who wants to wait a week when they miss a train? Although it was short-lived, the *Golden Gate Special* was a train not easily forgotten.

LEFT: The *Golden Gate Special*, promoted as "The Finest Train in the World," carried passengers from the Midwest to the San Francisco Bay Area in luxurious style.

ABOVE: *The most plush and luxurious of all railroad cars in the United States were the specially built private cars for railroad moguls and other rich businessmen. These cars were the equivalent of a modern-day private jet plane. This car, named Alexander, was built for the president of the Philadelphia & Reading, A. A. McLeod.*

The Union Pacific catered to the business traveler as well as to the tourist. To interest the discriminating businessman of 1915, Union Pacific and Chicago & North Western printed detailed advertisements describing the advantages of the *Overland* for business travelers. Particulars of the service were explained in technical railroad terms uncharacteristic of railroad travel brochures, which normally described train travel in more romantic language.

Overland Limited is making history. It gives a maximum of extra comforts for a minimum extra fare, $10. Businessmen en route can keep in close touch with important happenings of the world as well as their individual business. This train Saves a Business Day between Chicago and San Francisco. It is a businessman's train, with all the comforts and conveniences of one's own club. The new time schedule is 64 hours and 30 minutes.

Leaves Chicago daily at 7 p.m., from the new Passenger Terminal, Madison and Canal Streets, arrives San Francisco 9:30 a.m. third day.

It is the only exclusively first-class train, Chicago to San Francisco. The only daily extra-fare train, Chicago to California. It is a new train of new all-steel cars, with roomy berths, spacious drawing-rooms and compartments, barber shop, baths, stenographer, valet, ladies' maid, and excellent dining-car service.

Over a magnificent double-track system of one-hundred-pound steel rails, ballasted with Dustless Sherman Gravel, guarded every inch of the way by Automatic Electric Safety Signals.

In the early years, *Overland*'s illustrious passengers were carried in elegant Pullman Palace cars. Many cars were named in honor of points along the line. Some were named for big towns such as Oakland, California; others for more obscure points such as Alazon, Nevada. Little more than a connection between Southern Pacific and Western Pacific tracks with a few switching shacks and a sign, the town of Alazon possesses little of any real interest. (The origin of the name "Alazon," which is Latin for "braggart" or "boaster," is not known.) Other cars played off the *Overland* theme: most obviously the *Overview* and the *Overton*. Traditionally Pullman cars were painted a dark olive green, known as Pullman Green, with gold-leaf lettering.

Overland Wrecked in a Snowstorm

The winter of 1916–17 was particularly fierce in the open plains of Nebraska and Wyoming. Although the railroad took every precaution to keep the tracks clear of snow and safe for passenger trains, there were occasional problems. Snow and high winds can cause total "white out" conditions where visibility is nearly zero; drifts can pile snow higher than the tops of trains. Such extreme conditions can spell disaster for operating crews, and in the early morning hours of December 19, 1916, train No. 1 was involved in a serious collision during such a blizzard. A clipping titled "Wrecked in Storm" from the Laramie *Republican*, reprinted in Lucius Beebe's book *The Overland Limited*, reported the details of the mishap:

SNOWPLOW CRASHES INTO OBSERVATION CAR OF OVERLAND LIMITED PASSENGER TRAIN AT LOOKOUT IN NIGHT . . .

A disastrous wreck occurred near Lookout at about 1 o'clock this morning, when a snow plow ran into the rear observation car of train No. 1, the Overland Limited, one of the finest trains in the west and the finest on the Union Pacific, fortunately no one being hurt. The car was demolished and the snow plow was put out of commission.

The lateness of the hour for the rear end collision at Lookout, at which time the observation car was empty, made the injuries of no consequence. The observation car was almost on

top of the snow plow, and the cars were so tightly wedged together that it took some time to pull them apart. The track was blocked for several hours.

Country's Worst Storm

Trainmen state that the storm at and around Lookout last night was one of the worst ever experienced there, rendering the operation of trains very difficult. From the reports received here, a freight train just ahead of the Overland Limited was stalled in the snow, and No. 1 was compelled to stop for the freight. The snow plow, coming right behind, could not see the passenger train in time to avoid the collision, the wreck resulting.

General Manager W. M. Jeffers, who was in an official car attached to train No. 9, left his car here and hastened to the scene of the wreck on No. 17, and was in charge of the clearing of the track. He was joined later by Superintendent Bell, Assistant Superintendent Woodruff and other officials of the division. The trains from the west used the eastbound track and there was little delay on account of the wreck.

In the 1930s, a disaster of a very different sort befell a famous passenger while traveling aboard the *Overland*. Lucius Beebe also relays this tale.

. . . Ethel Barrymore, who invariably traveled in the grand manner of an earlier generation and occupied two drawing rooms banked with flowers and furnished with her own soft pillows and framed portraits of royal personages all arranged by her personal maid, got a nasty turn on re-entering her suite after an excursion to the diner. In passing through Chicago she had put up at the Ambassador Hotel whose proprietor, the celebrated Ernie Byfield, had presented her, along with more substantial refreshments for the voyage, with a couple of samples of his latest proprietary product called College Inn Tomato Juice Cocktails. Tomato juice was just emerging on the national awareness as a morning after restorative and the Byfield version, being in its early stages of manufacture, had been imperfectly processed. In Miss Barrymore's absence the containers had exploded spattering the drawing room with a reasonable facsimile of human gore. Her shrieks of dismay brought the train crew running and it took considerable persuasion to reassure her that a sensational murder hadn't been committed in her absence.

ABOVE: *The* Overland Limited *offered the best in luxury travel, and at the time that this poster was printed made the trip from Chicago to San Francisco in under seventy-two hours.*

THE DIESEL TAKES THE WEST

Diesel-electric locomotives had made flashy appearances on streamlined passenger trains, beginning with the Burlington's *Pioneer Zephyr* and Union Pacific's *City of Salina* in 1934. Prior to that, boxy diesel-electric switchers could be found prowling in freight yards, and self-propelled, gas-electric cars called "Doodlebugs" had been seen since the 1920s. Some Western railroads dabbled in electric power: the Southern Pacific had electrified some of its "commute" lines in the Bay Area, and Great Northern used electric power through its long Cascade Tunnel. The Milwaukee Road's hundreds of miles of Pacific Extension electrification was legendary. But the tried-and-true steam locomotive pulled most of the trains, freight and passenger alike. It was the steam locomotive that made the railroad a practical form of transportation, and it was the steam locomotive upon which railroads relied to move their trains. Talk of grand electrification schemes came and went. Sure, a few colorful diesels whisked fancy passenger trains across the countryside. But when it came down to running trains—real trains, long and heavy revenue freights—no diesel could do the job. Not, that is, until Electro-Motive Corporation (later General Motors' Electro-Motive Division) introduced the FT.

In 1939, Electro-Motive Corporation's demonstrator FT set—an experimental, streamlined, four-unit diesel (two A-unit cabs, and two B-unit boosters)—raised the eyebrows of railroad managers throughout the West and across the nation. What was so special about this new diesel? It was the first diesel-electric locomotive that offered significant tractive effort with reasonable operating speed; reliable, consistent service; relatively low maintenance; and that could be purchased in quantity at reasonable cost. The standard set of four units was rated at 5,400 horsepower; each unit had four axles powered by a 567 series, V16 diesel engine that generated 1,359 horsepower. Altogether this amounted to a maximum tractive effort of 228,000 pounds (103,512kg)—roughly equivalent of the state-of-the-art, articulated compound steam locomotives of the day. The FT was geared for seventy-five miles per hour (121kph) operation and carried enough fuel for roughly five hundred miles (805km) of operation, which allowed far fewer fueling stops than the steamers. The FT matched or outperformed its external combustion competition. A locomotive revolution was in the making.

Soon Electro-Motive was swamped with orders for its shining star. But FT dominance in the new locomotive market was interrupted in 1942 because of wartime demands on heavy machinery. Once restrictions began to let up, the

railroads placed orders for FTs as quickly as Electro-Motive's La Grange, Illinois, plant could pump them out. While Eastern railroads such as the Boston & Maine and the Erie Railroad operated FTs, it was in the West that the FT had the greatest impact. The Santa Fe had the largest fleet—roughly twenty-five percent of the total FT production, some 320 cabs and boosters—which allowed it to almost completely eliminate steam operations and dieselize its desert lines between Winslow, Arizona, and Barstow, California. This section of railroad had long been an operating hassle because it lacked the good water needed for steam locomotives. Diesels were the perfect solution. The Great Northern took delivery of the second largest fleet, nearly one hundred FT cabs and boosters. The Burlington had more than sixty; the Milwaukee Road more than fifty; and Northern Pacific, Rio Grande, and Rock Island all owned sizable fleets.

Ten years after the FT made its debut, the last commercially built steam locomotive rolled off the production line, and Electro-Motive was the leading producer of new locomotives in the United States.

OPPOSITE: Five modern diesel-electrics lead a westbound Santa Fe train through the Tehachapi Mountains of California.
BELOW: In 1934, the Burlington debuted its *Pioneer Zephyr*, the

first diesel-electric-powered streamlined passenger train. This three-car stainless-steel speedster toured the United States before entering regular passenger service. By the end of the 1930s, the Burlington had a whole fleet of Zephyr streamliners racing across the Midwest. **PAGES 68–69:** In the 1930s, streamlined trains were the latest fad to attract public attention. Initially, streamliners were designed to reduce wind resistance when operating at high speeds, although many later streamliners were styled primarily for aesthetic appeal. On March 11, 1939, some locals inspect an oil-burning steam-turbine-electric. This was an experimental General Electric locomotive design intended to rival the performance of the diesel-electric, but it never caught on.

CHAPTER THREE

RAILROADING IN COLORADO

OPPOSITE: *The Rio Grande operated a network of three-foot (91cm) gauge lines in Colorado, New Mexico, and Utah. Rio Grande No. 318, a 2-8-0 Consolidation-type locomotive, leads a freight near Durango, Colorado.*

WAR IN THE ROYAL GORGE

In the late 1850s, gold was discovered in Colorado, and soon the state was experiencing the same explosive growth as California a decade earlier. By the 1860s, the citizens of the budding city of Denver, Colorado, expected that their town would be accorded a premier status along the proposed transcontinental railroad. Situated at the foot of the Front Range, Denver was the largest settlement in Colorado, having grown up around the gold mining in the region. But in 1866, when Union Pacific's General Dodge explored a route west of Denver for his railroad, he was not impressed with what he found. A particularly unpleasant experience with a sudden Colorado blizzard sealed the issue: he would take his railroad elsewhere.

The people of Denver were outraged, horrified, and dismayed when the route of the Union Pacific's transcontinental line bypassed their city in favor of an easier grade to the north through Cheyenne, Wyoming. They felt they had been wronged. Denver had expected to become a big railroad town, and had hoped to enjoy all the advantages of becoming one. Railroad towns were among the most prosperous of the era. Quality

RIGHT: *General William Jackson Palmer was a strong proponent of narrow-gauge railways, and he dreamed of a three-foot gauge empire connecting Denver with Mexico City.*

Palmer was noted for his amazing stamina and his ability to overcome adversity. While building the Kansas Pacific, he succeeded in constructing one hundred fifty miles (241km) of railroad in just ninety-two days, an impressive achievement by any standard.

After completing the Kansas Pacific, General Palmer began to dream on his own. He envisioned a railroad that would connect Denver and Mexico City. In 1870 he resigned from the Kansas Pacific and formed his own railroad, the Denver & Rio Grande. On his honeymoon in Wales, Great Britain, Palmer was impressed with the narrow-gauge lines he saw in operation there, and decided that slim gauge was the way to go. He chose the three-foot (91cm) standard for his Denver & Rio Grande, rather than the established North American standard gauge of 4 feet, 8½ inches (143cm). The advantages of the smaller gauge were clearly evident in mountain territory. Smaller locomotives and rolling stock cost less to build and operate. However, the largest savings were realized through substantially less costly construction practices. Narrow-gauge lines negotiate sharper curves, ascend steeper grades, and use shorter ties and lighter rail than standard-gauge lines.

Construction began on July 28, 1871, and a few months later the line was finished as far as Colorado Springs. The first official train on the Denver & Rio Grande operated from Denver to Colorado Springs on October 26, 1871. At first the railroad operated with seven locomotives: four 2-4-0s for passenger service and three large 2-6-0 Mogul-types for freight service. All were built by the Baldwin Locomotive Works in Pennsylvania. The Panic of 1873 slowed the railroad's construction efforts, but by 1876 its rails reached El Moro, near Trinidad, Colorado. Palmer hoped that here he could tap into the lucrative traffic moving over the Santa Fe Trail.

In its early days, the Denver & Rio Grande had difficulty raising sufficient funds for construction, and visible progress was often very slow. Conflicting destination goals also presented problems. Initially General Palmer wished to build a line over Raton Pass into New Mexico to Santa Fe, and then south to Mexico City. However, distractions kept luring Palmer away from his goal. The promise of lucrative traffic nearby had him building branches to Canon City and up over Le Veta Pass to reach the San Luis Valley. He kept looking farther westward, too. Mining communities high in the Colorado Rockies were unearthing valuable minerals and lots of traffic potential. The

transportation, the most obvious advantage, was just a beginning. Union Pacific placated Denver by agreeing to build a branch there south from Cheyenne. Called the Denver Pacific, this spur rolled into town in spring of 1870. Denver's first train was led by a diminutive locomotive prophetically named the *David H. Moffat*. Moffat was to be responsible for a considerable amount of railroad building in Colorado. Moreover, after the turn of the century, Moffat built the Denver & Salt Lake—an incredible line up and over the Front Range—in a costly attempt to place Denver on a transcontinental route.

A few months after the Denver Pacific arrived, a line from Kansas City to Denver was finished. First known as Union Pacific's Eastern Division, this line is better known by its later name, the Kansas Pacific. The driving force behind the construction of the Kansas Pacific was Gen. William Jackson Palmer, a talented Civil War veteran who had learned the art of railroading working for the Pennsylvania Railroad before the war. General

LEFT: *Palmer's Denver & Rio Grande vied with the Santa Fe for passage through the deep and narrow Royal Gorge; armed railroad employees met here, and before the dispute was settled blood was shed.*

ABOVE: *To maintain a constant grade in the mountains, tracks often had to take a less than direct route by looping around to follow the contours of the land.*

logical route west was just west of Canon City, through a deep, narrow cleft called the Royal Gorge of the Arkansas River. This deep river canyon was only thirty feet (9m) wide in places, two thousand feet (610m) deep, and so steep that there was no obvious place to walk, let alone build a railroad. Construction would be tricky and expensive.

Slow progress and Palmer's cavalier treatment of communities along the prospective route generated more antagonism and antipathy toward the Denver & Rio Grande than financial support. Anemic financing limited Palmer's ability to push his line through. Then came another threat to Denver & Rio Grande's

progress: in the early 1870s, when General Palmer began building south, he was the only show in town. But by 1876, the Atchison, Topeka & Santa Fe had completed its line across Kansas and reached Pueblo, deep into Denver & Rio Grande territory. The Santa Fe was aiming in the same direction as the Denver & Rio Grande. When General Palmer realized that the Santa Fe might soon secure a line through the narrow confines of Raton Pass, he sent his construction forces to occupy that strategic point. He was outwitted and outmaneuvered by Santa Fe forces directed by William Barstow Strong and led by Albert A. Robinson. Strong ordered Robinson to push a line over Raton

Pass, by armed force if necessary. Robinson's men beat the Denver & Rio Grande forces to the pass by only a few hours, securing the line for the Santa Fe. There was no other route south; the low crossing at Raton presented the only logical crossing of the Rockies in the region. The Denver & Rio Grande was shut out of the route.

Even as the Santa Fe and Denver & Rio Grande were vying for control of Raton, another situation was developing. In 1874 silver had been discovered at California Gulch, otherwise known as Leadville, Colorado. For several years this discovery was not widely known, but in 1878 vast quantities of silver began to be extracted from the mines around Leadville. Overnight this tiny Colorado community exploded into the latest Western boomtown. The traffic potential was enormous. General Palmer wanted to guarantee that he could secure a line to Leadville before his rival. He quickly shifted his interest and resources toward his Western route, eyeing the Royal Gorge.

Santa Fe also wanted to tap Leadville's riches, and soon both railroads were building toward that narrow rock canyon. The rivalry between the two companies was fierce and both sides hired gun-toting thugs to accompany the grading crews. Soon a battle was raging, although mostly in courtrooms. Santa Fe had favor with regional courts, and Denver & Rio Grande lost there, but Santa Fe's victory was short-lived. Denver & Rio Grande had favor with federal courts. In the middle of the legal battle, an awkward compromise was reached between the two companies, and Santa Fe leased the Rio Grande. This was a tenuous truce at best. General Palmer still retained some authority over his railroad, and Santa Fe did not abide by the rules of the lease. When the federal courts ruled in favor of Denver & Rio Grande, Palmer sought to reclaim the sovereignty of his railroad.

Armed Denver & Rio Grande forces, sometimes accompanied by local sheriffs, took back the Rio Grande from the Santa Fe. In some places, Santa Fe employees abandoned the railroad without a fight. But others dug in and defended their positions. When Rio Grande men attempted to reclaim the train dispatcher's office in Pueblo, Colorado, they were met by a hail of bullets. Furthermore, Santa Fe tough Bat Masterson barricaded himself in the Pueblo roundhouse and fired upon the Denver & Rio Grande army with a Gatling gun. Eventually Rio Grande convinced him to vacate through financial persuasion.

The situation in the Royal Gorge would not be resolved so easily. The bandits hired by both parties were hungry for blood and accustomed to a wild, dangerous lifestyle. Both sides constructed stone fortresses and a bloody guerrilla war was conducted. Before the courts brought peace, as many as twenty men had lost their lives in what was one of the bloodiest "corporate" wars on record. The Denver & Rio Grande held the Royal Gorge and pushed their narrow-gauge line through to Leadville, though for a short time the Gorge had dual-gauge tracks for both railroads.

Rio Grande's three-foot-gauge (91cm) lines soon covered much of central and southwestern Colorado, with the mainline extending clear through to Salt Lake City. In later years the Rio Grande mainline through the Royal Gorge was converted to standard gauge and hosted the famous *Scenic Limited*, which would pause in the narrow gorge to allow passengers to enjoy the splendid scenery.

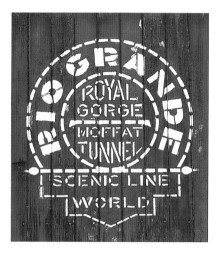

ABOVE: *In later years the Rio Grande boasted of its scenic route through the famous Royal Gorge. However, in 1997, after several railroad mergers, the route was deemed redundant and is now threatened with abandonment.*

RIO GRANDE SOUTHERN

In the annals of Colorado railroads, more than a mention has to be made of one of its least likely lines, the Rio Grande Southern, the vision of Otto Mears. Despite protests from those who said it was impossible to build a railroad in the high, remote regions of southwest Colorado, he completed his Rio Grande Southern in a relatively short time. The impetus was simple: the prosperous silver mines around Telluride. With support from the Denver & Rio Grande, which connected to the Rio Grande Southern at both ends, construction began in the autumn of 1889. The line was built at a furious pace and was completed by December 1891. Its 162-mile (261km) route was among the most incredible ever conceived. It traversed the legendary Lizard Head Pass at a towering elevation of 10,250 feet (3,124m) above sea level, wound through the hair-raising Ophir Loops atop spindly wooden trestles, and crossed the Dallas Divide at 8,989 feet (2,740m). Much of its three-foot-gauge (91cm) line featured formidably steep 4-percent grades—the bane and dread of operating crews.

OPPOSITE: *The Baldwin-built Montezuma had the honor of hauling the Rio Grande's first passenger train. In its early days the Rio Grande employed four diminutive 2-4-0 locomotives in passenger service. The Rio Grande used 36-inch (91cm) gauge track as opposed to the 4-foot, ½-inch (123cm) "standard" gauge used by most American railroads.*

To this near-fantasy railroad, author Lucius Beebe provides a marvelous context. In his book *Narrow Gauge in the Rockies*, he wrote:

> *When in years to come, men shall name the names of sparkling romance that are the lexicon of the Old West, the names that clutch at the heart and have entered the stream of the nation's consciousness, the Alamo, Tombstone, Dodge City, the Staked Plains, Santa Fe Trail, South Pass, Union Pacific, Deadwood, Wells Fargo and Virginia City, they will be advised to include in that valiant tally, the name of Otto Mears's masterpiece, the lonely, desolate and perhaps futile but still transcendingly triumphant Rio Grande Southern Railroad.*

What was so special about Rio Grande Southern? Why is this peculiar line venerated above the many miles of Colorado mountain railroad? What mystique did it hold? Lucius Beebe answers as follows:

> *Here were concentrated all the basic realities of mountain railroading in primeval times: the thirty-pound rail laid without ballast on the elemental earth, rights of way cleaving to ledges above the bottomless abyss, snowsheds, loops, stub switches, the little mixed train daily and the teapot locomotives driven against all probability and the elements by the old bearded eagle eyes of legend.*

The Rio Grande Southern was not just any small railroad winding its way among rocky crags and over mountain passes; it was the very bread that railroad legends are served on.

By the time the Rio Grande Southern was nearing completion, the tradition of last-spike ceremonies had been firmly established in the United States. The little town of Rico, Colorado, would not be outdone by the Promontorys and Gold Creeks of other, more prominent lines. Never mind that the railroad had yet to connect its two ends. The completion of the railroad to Rico was reason enough for bold celebration, and on October 15, 1891, special trains filled with dignitaries and sightseers rolled into Rico. The townspeople had decorated as never before. Flags and bunting added a thrill of festivity. A brass band came up from Telluride. A crowd assembled, and an inscribed spike was driven. This spike was not gold, it was silver in honor

of the ore the line would soon carry in plentiful abundance. The inscriptions on the spike offered tribute to both the man and the commodity that made the narrow, diminutive rails over the mountains possible: "The Honorable Otto Mears, President" and "Silver from the Enterprise Mine."

After a hearty banquet and fashionable feasting, the celebrities left town. The final miles were completed during the next two months, and on December 19, 1891, the line was truly finished.

In the first year and a half of operation, the Rio Grande Southern enjoyed the greatest prosperity of its existence. Silver ore and coal flowed over the rails in great quantity. In these prosperous times, the crews were reasonably well compensated. Locomotive

engineers were paid three dollars a day, and if they served for a full year, their pay was increased to four dollars a day. Firemen were not as well compensated; they only received $2.40 per day.

But Rio Grande Southern's prosperity was short-lived. The Panic of 1893 swept many of the nation's best-known railroads—Western giants Northern Pacific and Union Pacific among them—into insolvency. The Panic also caught the tiny Rio Grande Southern. For a while during its bankruptcy it was unable to pay its employees, and then the railroad had to enforce a twenty percent pay cut. Because of Rio Grande Southern's difficulties, Denver & Rio Grande forced out the line's esteemed president and assumed control.

While in the early days Rio Grande Southern owned an array of interesting equipment, its most intriguing feature was its difficult mountain operation. Rio Grande Southern's legendary reputation was built from stories generated during the course of its daily operations. The burden of toil placed on the men of the Rio Grande Southern has no comparison in modern American life. And while the company's disregard for the comfort of its employees and its cavalier treatment of them were not unusual for the time period—hardy men were expected to do without basic necessities like food and sleep—the situation of their employment was extraordinary. This was mountain railroading, and anyone with a weak constitution might just as well seek easier employment elsewhere. Under normal conditions, bringing a train from station to station was an ordeal; but in bad weather this could become an adventure, if not an endurance test. Failure of such a test was perilous indeed.

Josie Moore Crum chronicles these perils in *The Rio Grande Southern Railroad*, a priceless treasure for those interested in Western railroad operations. Her husband, John Harvey Crum, was one of those wild men in the pioneering days of Colorado railroading who ran trains on the Rio Grande Southern. Operations on the Telluride Branch in 1907 give a feeling for the daily hardship endured by the railroad's crews.

The duty of this crew was to switch the Pandora and Telluride yards, carry ore to Vance Junction for the maintrains to pick up and bring back coal, mining machinery, lumber and living supplies. Then, when the mainline crews had more than they could

do [the branch crew] would take a train to the top of Lizard Head Pass or to the top of Dallas Divide.

Much ore was loaded and much switching was done in the Pandora yard. The following incident is representative of a common trouble there—ice on the rail. An engine was stuck. Barney Cornelius, the hog head, kept rocking it back and forth trying to get it to move one way or the other but could get no results. Meanwhile the fireman had gotten down and crawled up on a pile of lumber. Finally the engineer, after leaving the throttle open and the reversing lever in the forward position, got down and crawled up on another pile of lumber. The conductor and one brakeman were standing on the ground while the other brakeman was in a gondola just back of the engine. Unnoticed by anybody the wheels wore the ice down and the locomotive started with a bang. All four men began yelling and motioning to this second brakeman to do something about stopping the runaway. He clambered over the tender and down into the cab; then he shut off the throttle and applied the brakes. The critter stopped.

It was only after a full day's work at Telluride and Pandora that the crew was called for a mainline trip. The requirements were that the brakemen should ride on the tops of the cars no matter how bad the wind or weather or how many hours they had been on duty. They had to stand up, which position was called "decorating." One night a tired brakeman went to sleep, dropped his lantern and tumbled himself, but caught onto something and didn't fall off.

From 1890 to 1908 there was no limit on the number of hours men could be worked, 48 or more not being out of the ordinary. The word "rest" was beyond the lexicon of the railroad company. It was common practice to call a crew that had not more than an hour's rest after a 30-hour trip to go out on another run.

In 1909 most of the Lizard Head snowshed with a number of cars and a lot of track burned and both passenger trains were caught on the south side. The Branch crew every morning took the baggage, mail, express and passengers to Lizard Head which it transferred to the southbound passenger [train]. The crew returned, switched the rest of the day in the Telluride and Pandora yards and late in the afternoon went to Lizard Head again to effect the transfer of the same kinds of stuff but from the northbound passenger [train].

The Branch men, who were called for 6:30 A.M. and did not tie up until midnight or after, were getting not more than three or four hours of sleep in a day. According to the Sixteen-Hour Law that had recently gone into effect they were entitled to ten hours off duty if they had worked 16 hours. After several days of this, four of the men—Engineer Sam Davies, Fireman Frank Davies, Brakeman Harv Israel and Brakeman John Crum—could not stand any more and tied up for ten hours rest. . . . The Company retaliated by removing them from service. The management claimed it had a right to use men as much and as long as it pleased because this was a case of emergency. Mr. Ed Gamble, the agent at Telluride, took the matter up with the Company and proved that this was not a case of emergency as a relief crew could have been obtained. The Company, then, re-instated the men and paid them for lost time. This somewhat impeded, though did not stop, further attempts at abrogating the 16-hour law.

This country is in the highest precipitation district in Colorado. So, the worst annoyance Branch men had to deal with was being wet, continually wet. The overshoes of the time were cloth-topped, allright in dry snow but no good in wet snow or rain. The slickers were clumsy and inconvenient and admitted nearly as much moisture as they kept out. To top all else, one day's soggy attire had no chance to dry when it had to be donned the next day.

THE GALLOPING GOOSE

The 1930s were tough on railroads, particularly small railroads like Rio Grande Southern in southwestern Colorado. The advent of the automobile and the Great Depression had deprived Rio Grande Southern of much of its passenger business. To survive it had to cut its costs dramatically. Many other smaller lines had similar problems and looked to cut passenger train operating costs by running less expensive trains.

THE GALLOPING GOOSE

Railroads had been experimenting with self-propelled internal combustion motor railcars since the beginning of the century. McKeen's famous windsplitter was one example. Gas-electric railcars known as Doodlebugs became popular in the 1920s. These cars used a gasoline engine to generate electricity that powered electric-traction motors. They were in essence self-propelled trolley cars. Many railroads large and small employed them in branch-line passenger service.

Railcar construction became a competitive business. The J. G. Brill company of Philadelphia, a giant in the production of electric trolley cars and electric interurbans, found the rail motor car business a natural extension of its market. In the 1920s and 1930s, another company, the Electro-Motive Corporation (later a subsidiary of General Motors), made its reputation by

building rail motor cars. It advertised the operating economy of motor cars and challenged railroad managers to study the numbers. To save the managers time it provided elaborate calculations: the Electro-Motive Corporation demonstrated that its motor cars cost only fifty-five cents per mile to operate in passenger service, a dramatic savings over traditional steam trains, which cost eighty-six cents per mile.

If heavyweight rail motor cars were not to a railroad's liking, they could try railbuses. These were essentially motorbuses, the sort found on the roads, that ran on rails with flanged wheels. Railbus engines employed a direct drive and were smaller than most motor car engines. Many firms built railbuses, including A. Meister & Sons in Sacramento, California; White Motor Company of Cleveland, Ohio; and streetcar companies like Brill.

ABOVE: *By the 1930s, the Rio Grande Southern was chronically short of funds. It wanted to buy railbuses to reduce the cost of running passenger services, but could not afford to buy them. Instead it built its own railbuses, which came to be known as Galloping Geese.*

OPPOSITE: *Galloping Goose No. 7 is between Ridgway and Dolores, Colorado, on its first run. It was home-built by the railroad in 1936 using the body of a Ford.*

BELOW: *By the early 1950s, Rio Grande Southern was near the end of the line. In 1950 and 1951, it tried running its popular Galloping Geese in passenger excursion service, but the effort failed, and the railroad folded in 1952. If it had survived it would now be heralded as a national treasure.*

Rio Grande Southern Railroad
PIERPONT FULLER, Receiver

THE "GALLOPING GOOSE"

THE "GALLOPING GOOSE" LINE
Most spectacular narrow-gauge railroad in America!

Offers you your most exciting railroad adventure!

See the gorgeous San Juan country, snow-capped 14-thousand-foot peaks, dashing trout streams, wild flower timberline paradise, historic gold and silver mines.

THE "GALLOPING GOOSE" beginning on or about June 15, 1950, will operate for excursion and sightseeing trips in the San Juan Basin of Southwestern Colorado.

ONE-DAY ROUND TRIPS:
1. Ridgway to Telluride famous gold and silver mining camp. $4.50
2. Ridgway to Lizzard Head Pass via spectacular Ophir Loop and Trout Lake. $5.25
3. Durango to Dolores, via Thompson Park and beautiful mesa country. $6.00
4. Dolores to Lizzard Head Pass, through the magnificent Dolores River Canon and famous silver mining camp at Rico. $5.00

HALF-DAY ROUND TRIP:
Durango to Mancos over colorful high mesa country. $4.00

Longer trips, overnight trips or special charter trips may be arranged. Federal tax not included in quoted rates. Children under 12 one-half fare.

Reservations should be made well in advance as a minimum of ten full fare tickets will be required for each trip.

For reservations or further information write or telephone Rio Grande Southern Railroad office at Durango, Dolores or Ridgway, Colorado.

While other railroads studied the advertising and purchased motor cars and railbuses, narrow-gauge Rio Grande Southern had to make more frugal choices. It had entered its second receivership and could not justify the cost of even the most inexpensive commercial rail motor cars. Instead, it decided to build its own. The Rio Grande Southern had dabbled in internal combustion contraptions back in 1913, when the general superintendent, W. D. Lee, converted a secondhand Ford automobile into a self-propelled rail inspection car. He had attached flanged wheels set to the line's thirty-six-inch (91cm) gauge, eliminated the steering mechanism, and equipped it with a large prominent exterior sunshade—in reality an extension of the awkward canopy that served as the roof. With this funky conveyance, on which was proudly lettered R. G. S. No. 1, Lee traveled around the railroad solving problems and attending to official business.

Josie Moore Crum, in her book *The Rio Grande Southern Railroad*, relates how the railroad's receiver, Victor Miller decided to cut the railroad's passenger deficit by using railbuses. Between 1926 and 1932, most of the railroad's revenue had dried up. Miller had been appointed receiver by a federal court in 1929. He realized that costs must be cut on the small line. Steam-powered passenger trains were simply too expensive to operate. When buying new buses from a commercial manufacturer proved too expensive he instead followed the precedent of Lee's home-built inspection car and had the railroad construct a small fleet of railbuses to its own design. He enlisted the help of Rio Grande Superintendent Forest White and Chief Mechanic Jack Odenbaugh, and in June 1931 the first Rio Grande Southern railbus entered service. Crum quotes Miller's description of the homemade contraption:

> *A seven-passenger automobile sedan of Pierce Arrow manufacture, model 33, of the year of 1926, is spread in the body to the ordinary width of a narrow-gauge car to a carrying capacity of ten passengers with the chassis remodeled to fit two four-wheel trucks of 36 inch gauge; a light metal trailer of box car character and a capacity in excess of ten tons, running on a third narrow-gauge four-wheel truck, is permanently affixed to the rear of the automobile. The aggregate vehicle then runs as one unit on three sets of narrow-gauge trucks, of which the wheels of the second are drivers. It is equipped with power brakes, special headlights and bells. Overall length is 44 feet, outside width*

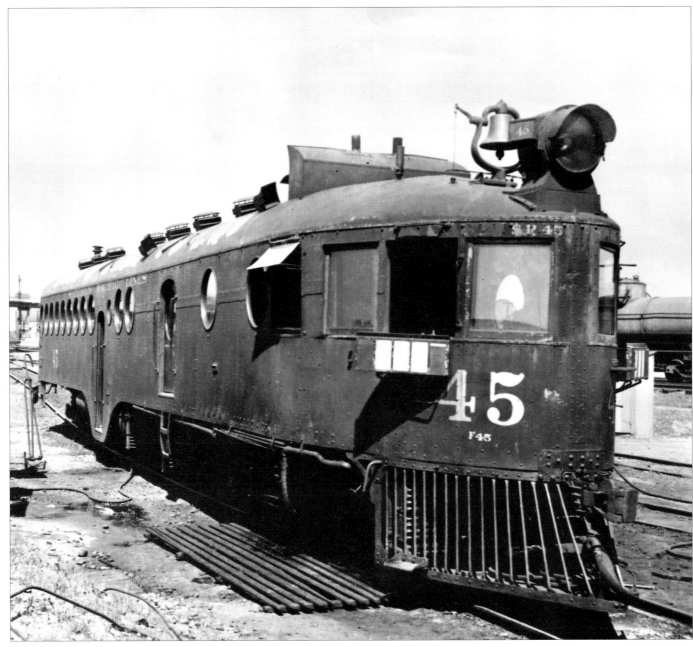

7 ½ feet, length of van 24 feet, total weight 14,800 pounds, schedule speed 20 miles per hour, average gasoline consumption 5 ½ miles per gallon and average cost of operation 15 cents per mile in summer.

The first Rio Grande Southern railbus was completed in June 1931 at a cost of $850.00; the second bus, which was somewhat more substantial, was completed in August 1931 and cost $1,740.00. By 1936 Miller had a fleet of seven buses, and an eighth bus was built for the San Cristobal Railroad.

These curious silver railbuses quickly changed the character of passenger business on the railroad. And, while they cut oper-

ating costs, they were not universally liked. Awkward and clumsy-looking, they were a world away from the elaborately decorated trains of old. In fact, one disgruntled railroad observer graced the buses with the name "Galloping Goose," as they and the Rio Grande Southern are forever remembered. Crum relates:

Mr. F. B. Wilson, proprietor of the Busy Corner Pharmacy at Telluride and once general time inspector for the R. G. S., tells how the Galloping Goose acquired its name. Nicholas Schools was the superintendent of the Western Colorado Power Company generating plant at Ilium. Mrs. Schools always called Mr. Wilson on the phone when the passenger trains, and later the buses, pased Ilium. The latter, then, notified the hotel which ran a cab to passenger trains at that time, the men who carried the mail to the post office and the paper delivery boys. Mrs. Schools very much disliked the busses because they had displaced the passenger trains. One time, probably around 1932, she called Mr. Wilson and said:

"I see that thing coming up the track."

"What thing?" he inquired.

"Aw," she said, "that contraption that looks like a Galloping Goose."

The name stuck. Soon the Rio Grande Southern, which had previously been known as the "Silver San Juan Scenic Line," became the "Galloping Goose Line." And an insignia of a goose was proudly applied to the buses. Lucius Beebe states in *Narrow Gauge in the Rockies*, "Whether it was its wildly improbable name or valiant enlistment in a lost cause that attracted sympathetic attention, the Galloping Goose became in its lifetime a Colorado institution of the first magnitude." At times, a swaying, fully

loaded Goose clambering up the steep grades of Lizard Head Pass may have more resembled an African safari vehicle than a piece of American railroad equipment.

The new Galloping Geese virtually eliminated the need for steam-powered passenger trains on the Rio Grande Southern, though steam continued to haul freight. Most of the time the Galloping Geese bounced along the steep 4-percent grades of Rio Grande Southern quite happily. However, they were not sure-footed in ice and snow. Operation in the winter months occasionally led to some harrowing experiences. Other mishaps were attributed to inadequate braking. Lucius Beebe, always one to embellish details for the sake of a good story, eloquently implies that other mishaps may have been the careless result of overzealous operators.

Occasionally, a Galloping Goose driven furiously in an effort to keep schedule down a four percent grade, got out of hand and imitated its prototype in everything but actual flight. When at last its mad progress left the rails, the entire contrivance

BELOW: *At the very end of their active careers, several of the Galloping Geese were converted for excursion service by equipping the freight and express area at the rear of the vehicle with recycled trolley-car seats.*

Rather than being discarded as scrap, No. 4 was repaired and soldiered on for several more years. After World War II it was reengined with a war surplus GMC motor.

Crum tells of another runaway Goose, also in the spring of 1945. This one was going north toward Ridgway with passengers and had been running very late. The driver, a man named Cooper, was about to "go dead on the law." In those days railroad employees could work a maximum of sixteen hours, after which they had to be relieved by law. So the railroad dispatched Master Mechanic Lee Elwell to intercept the wayward Goose, relieve Mr. Cooper, and bring them to their destination. Elwell caught up with the bus at the Dallas Divide and assumed operation. As soon as he started down the grade he found the brakes would not hold. It did not take long before they knew the Goose was out of control. The difference between a safe ride and a wild one on a steep grade can be a matter of just a few seconds, and an experienced operator knows when it is too late, often long before the inevitable crash comes.

Lee Elwell was quick to note the lack of braking ability and, fearing the worst, ordered his passengers and Cooper to jump from the speeding Goose. He, too, jumped, but despite his fears, the Goose did not plunge into a ravine. Instead, after its human crew and passengers had departed, the brakes began to grip, and it rolled safely into Ridgway with no one on board!

The heavy mountain snow could play real havoc with the lightweight Geese. No doubt the thought of riding one through avalanche territory discouraged some patrons, but the railroad needed to meet its schedules and dispatched the Geese even in tough conditions. Crum relates a story by W. G. Laube.

ABOVE: *Galloping Goose No. 4, which Dean Hainey rode down the Dallas Divide, is now preserved in downtown Telluride, Colorado.*

OPPOSITE: *Given their distinctive look, the Rio Grande Southern's home-built Galloping Geese railbuses are not likely to be confused with anything else that ran on steel wheels. Goose No. 2 is now preserved at the Colorado Railroad Museum in Golden.*

disintegrated like a powder mill exploding and a reserve Goose was dispatched to pick up the mails and the maimed from the hillside they occupied. The Galloping Geese inherited most of the thrills of mountain railroading in its most primitive state of development, but no fatalities were ever attributed to them.

Crum offers more accurate accounts of wild Geese in the Colorado Rockies. One tale is told by Goose operator Dean Hainey and gives a feel for the rigors of mountain railroading without imaginative embellishment.

On March 1, 1945, I started down Dallas Divide on the four percent with Motor No. 4. As I neared the crossing, the drive shaft broke and fell down on the ties, which bent it so that it whirled and broke the air line. This left me with a free wheeler. I rode the bus for about a mile and a half and it got to going so fast that I hung on the running board watching for a snow bank in which to land. I saw one and leaped. The bus kept on going for another half mile, then jumped the track at the spur now identified as Quist Junction, the place where the ore train piled up. When I got to the wreck I found the operator's cab to be demolished. Had I been in it I would have been in the same state.

On February 3, 1932, Dick Murphy started out of Telluride with the Rio Grande Southern's Streamliner [sic], "The Galloping Goose." It was storming badly and a light freight was sent ahead to break the trail. They found a number of small slides below Ophir and it took most of the day to get on down the hill. The "Goose" was close behind.

At a point along a steep hillside near Milepost 57 ½ a deluge of snow slid off the hill, completely burying the bus. Needless to say, the "Streamliner" came to an abrupt halt without any help from the brakes. Murphy was able to extricate himself by working the door in and out a number of times until he had made a gap large enough to reach out and start digging. The freight train had gone on to Coke Ovens, three miles farther, and while taking water noticed that the bus had failed to follow. The crew decided to back the train and look for it. In the meantime another slide had come down between the train and the bus.

Percy Cuddigan, the brakeman, started on foot to look for the missing bus and driver. When he arrived at the scene of the slide he found Murphy playing groundhog, digging himself out and up through the snow. He helped until Murphy was free and then the two walked to the freight train. They proceeded to Rico, leaving the U.S. mail in its cage safely buried under tons of snow until it could be dug out the next day.

The Goose was an invention of necessity, a vain effort to save a doomed railroad from an inevitable abandonment. Lucius Beebe quotes David Lavender: "Passenger traffic vanished first, of course; then trucks took the cattle and ore. And then the Goose came, that monstrous hybrid of an efficiency expert's mating with a balance sheet. It was high time to tear up the tracks and leave." Lavender was clearly a partisan of strict, old-fashioned railroading, done with steam locomotives and railroad cars.

Rio Grande Southern continued to operate its unique fleet of Galloping Geese into the 1950s. Clark Johnson, Jr., had the luck and privilege to catch a ride on one for the length of the line between Ridgway and Durango, including the Telluride branch where the station still stands, now a restaurant. Mr. Johnson notes:

…the Goose was uncomfortable, it was "springfree"—it had no noticeable suspension—and bounced along at about 30 miles an hour. Making matters worse I think they were still using 56 pound rail and the track was poorly maintained creating a really rough ride. But, the biggest drawback was the lack of a toilet. Instead the railroad had little outhouses spotted along the right-of-way at key locations. I know, because I had food poisoning and visited every one!

Of course the real tragedy is that the state of Colorado did not have the sense to preserve the line. It was a national treasure! A few years after I rode it, it was abandoned. The fools.

Today, though the line is gone, a few of the Galloping Geese are preserved. No. 4, which Dean Hainey rode down the Dallas Divide, is at Telluride, and another resides in Golden, Colorado.

CHAPTER FOUR

EMPIRES OF THE NORTH

OPPOSITE: *The Northern Pacific connected Minnesota's Twin Cities of Minneapolis and St. Paul with Portland, Oregon. This heavily decorated Northern Pacific train is likely destined for the railroad's last-spike ceremony at Gold Creek, Montana.*

HENRY VILLARD'S NORTHERN PACIFIC

Following the Civil War, the United States grew by leaps and bounds, and immigrants from the East Coast and all around the world increasingly looked toward the West. Oregon had aspirations of greatness. Portland, Oregon, was already a thriving northwestern port, vying with Puget Sound ports for dominance of regional trade. But Oregon struggled under geographical inferiority. California was graced with the Pacific Railroad, and new immigrants and businesses poured into the Golden State. But Oregon did not have its own railroad. And without a railroad, Oregon lay hopelessly off the beaten path, an unhappy and disconcerting situation for its residents and businesses. Promoters in places like the agriculturally rich Willamette Valley had great difficulty attracting settlers. Even when colorful brochures lured prospective immigrants to Oregon with promises of bountiful harvests and good living, newcomers often only got as far as California. "Why go on to Oregon, when all we could ever want is here?" an immigrating farmer might ask.

Without a railroad, travelers to Oregon had two tedious and time-consuming options. They could either take the traditional,

ABOVE: *Founded in 1835, Portland, Oregon, named after Portland, Maine, was the largest city in the Pacific Northwest until it was outranked by Seattle after 1900.*

overland route, like so many pioneers in the years before the Pacific Railroad, and trudge along the Oregon Trail in organized wagon trains (an unappealing prospect, since the trip would take months). Or they could take the train to California and then a steamship up along the coast to Portland. Either way, the journey would require far greater endurance than a trip to any number of enticing locations in California. This state of affairs had obvious implications. Oregon was less likely to prosper than its southern neighbor. In fact, Oregon might be entirely eclipsed as California prospered—certainly a most intolerable situation. Aggravating the situation was the Central Pacific Railroad, whose primary goal was to encourage California settlement. Its reasoning was very simple: more California settlers meant more goods and people to transport in the future, therefore more business. Central Pacific agents did little to direct travelers to the Pacific Northwest and likely encouraged many would-be Oregonians, Washingtonians, and others to remain in California. It was not only Oregon that suffered—though certainly its citizens were among the most vocal. All of the Pacific Northwest was neglected. But promoters for the region did not just sit idly by while the hordes of would-be settlers passed them up for golden fields and sunny shores to the south. Northwest promoters developed schemes and plans to attract, direct, and help

establish prospective settlers. Examples of the Northwest's rich soil were sent back east along with grain and other products in an effort to convince prospective settlers of the region's fertile potential. How could farmers pass up the opportunity to farm this great region? Advertisements were placed in European newspapers to promote the Northwest to potential settlers. Agents were established in several European cities and at key transportation hubs in the United States, such as New York and Omaha, in an effort to guide future Northwesterners to their new homes. Attracting new settlers was obviously the key to future prosperity.

California was not the only state competing with the Northwest for settlers. So were the bountiful states of Iowa, Nebraska, and Kansas in the Midwest, not to mention more established places like Wisconsin, Minnesota, and Illinois. An office was established in Topeka, Kansas, for the specific purpose of trying to persuade new immigrants who felt dissatisfied with Kansas to try the Pacific coast instead.

All the while, the Northwest awaited its own railroad.

The Northern Pacific

The northern route had long been under consideration for a transcontinental railroad. Even in the 1850s, early proponents of a railroad to the Pacific had looked at this route. But concerns about difficult operations in harsh winter weather and the ongoing strife between North and South dissuaded builders from seriously considering the northern route, and ultimately the central route was selected for the first transcontinental railroad. Yet the northern route would not languish too long. On July 2, 1864, only a couple of years after the authorization of the Pacific Railroad along the central route, President Lincoln authorized the Northern Pacific charter. Despite this relatively early start, the Northern Pacific did not enjoy the same rapid construction that propelled the Union Pacific and Central Pacific to completion in 1869. The Northern Pacific was beset with financial setbacks. The grants that enabled the Central Pacific and Union Pacific to complete their line were not available to the Northern Pacific. Not that Northern Pacific had no federal support—it was endowed with one of the largest state and federal land grants ever given to a private company. But it experienced great difficulty in turning its vast land grants—much of which existed in remote and desolate portions of the northern plains and Northwest—into capital. Land in the middle of nowhere, without a railroad to serve it, had very little value.

Philadelphia financier Jay Cooke, one of the most powerful and influential money brokers of the period, took an interest in the Northern Pacific and soon became its most ardent supporter. Cooke, enamored with the prospect of settlements and business in the Northwest, began an earnest campaign to promote the region. His Northwest promotions are the stuff of legend. Cooke went all out, heralding the Northwest as an undeveloped wonderland with a mild climate and land capable of producing bountiful harvest. His hyperbole induced some sarcastic critics to call the Northwest "Jay Cooke's Banana Belt."

Tracks were laid across Minnesota and into the Dakota territory, but then money ran out. Cooke's finance scheme stalled, and he was unable to attract continuing investment to keep the project rolling. He was stuck with large quantities of worthless paper bonds, an incomplete railroad, and little hope of generating revenue. His scheme had collapsed. His bankruptcy followed, an event that shook the financial world and led to the great Panic of 1873, at that time the worst financial depression the United States had ever seen. The result was a stagnation of railroad projects around the nation, especially in the Pacific Northwest.

Henry Villard

Henry Villard proved to be Northern Pacific's savior. Villard was an ambitious German with strong ties to the city of Portland, Oregon. During the late 1870s, he took a keen interest in the growing region's transportation network. His first railroad project was the Oregon Steamship & Navigation Company, which quickly became the Oregon Railway & Navigation Company under Villard. This company controlled most of the shipping in the region. To secure its dominant position, Villard began building a railroad eastward along the south bank of the great Columbia River.

Portland, desperate to maintain its supremacy in Northwest transportation and anxious to be the terminus of a northern transcontinental railroad, was nervously watching the slow—at times imperceptible—progress of the Northern Pacific. Would the Northern Pacific save Portland? Or ruin it? Portlanders viewed the Northern Pacific as a mixed blessing. Its route—designed to connect the Lake Superior port of Duluth with Puget Sound—would greatly enhance trade moving from the Pacific Northwest; as a whole, the region would undoubtedly prosper. However, many feared, justifiably, that this prosperity would come at Portland's expense.

As the largest port in the region, Portland enjoyed all the advantages of being the biggest show around. (Portland endured accusations of rate gouging and other abuses.) However, the Northern Pacific would not terminate at Portland, but at a new city, Tacoma, Washington, located on Puget Sound, with a harbor superior to that at Portland. Many believed that a great volume of ocean traffic handled through Portland would be diverted to Tacoma. Certainly if Portland wished to maintain its premier position, having the only railroad around serve another port was not acceptable. Portlanders grew even more wary as the Northern Pacific's routing schemes changed from time to time, and the proposed line to Portland sometimes appeared, but as a mere branch line. The main route, by one scheme, was to be built over the Washington Cascades. The reasons behind the Puget Sound bias were simple. The proposed harbor at Tacoma had distinct natural advantages over Portland, and, perhaps more important, many of the financial interests behind Northern Pacific had stakes in Tacoma's future development.

During the 1870s, various schemes for a transcontinental line to Oregon had been drafted and abandoned. One proposal arousing considerable interest was a route over the Oregon Cascades to connect with the Central Pacific at a town called Winnemucca, in central Nevada. This plan failed because of Central Pacific's more pressing California interests.

Villard knew the value of the coming railroad, and he was intent on Portland having its own transcontinental route, not just a branch off another port's line. So he planned to connect his Oregon Railway & Navigation line, which was to run across the northern tier of Oregon, with a Union Pacific line running north from Salt Lake City. Unfortunately, such a scheme looked easier than it was. First, Northern Pacific interests promised to foul Villard's plans. Second, he had grave concerns about Union Pacific's ambitions—it was controlled by the notorious rail

IMMIGRANT TRAINS OF THE NORTHERN PACIFIC

Northern Pacific embraced immigrants, enticing them, encouraging them, and persuading them to settle along its routes in the northern plains and Pacific Northwest. While there was a population center at each end of the Northern Pacific, much of the central portion of its route did not serve anyone, and thus only carried overhead traffic. When the Northern Pacific laid its rails across desolate plains and mountains, critics decried the railroad as folly. No one lived there. Without people to ride the line and ship goods, how could the line ever hope to make a profit? Yet, one of the principal reasons people in the Pacific Northwest had demanded the line be built was precisely to bring in immigrants. The region needed more people to survive. So the railroad had to run a vicious circle: since there were no people along its route, it had a difficult time generating the revenue it needed to build tracks; but because there was no railroad, immigrants were not inclined to settle in the Northwest.

Yet the railroad knew that immigrants were the future of the line. They would settle unpopulated regions, produce goods to ship over the rails, and become a solid ridership base. Northern Pacific had an even greater interest in promoting settlement along its lines than other Western railroads. To enable the building of the railroad, Congress had granted Northern Pacific large quantities of land in lieu of cash subsidy. Originally this totaled some sixty million acres (24,000,000ha) of land—the largest government land grant to a private company in history. But in the end Northern Pacific only claimed thirty-nine million acres (15,600,000ha) because it failed to complete its route on the mandated schedule. A fraction of Northern Pacific's land was used to construct the railroad. The remainder had to be sold to raise money. By encouraging settlement, the Northern Pacific secured both its own future and that of the region it served.

Beginning in the 1880s, the railroads, particularly the Northern Pacific, promoted the Northwest heavily. In addition to distributing literature, the railroads established immigration agencies in Great Britain and elsewhere in Europe. Promoters had clear racial biases and preferred settlers from northern European nations to those from most other parts of the world. Americans from the eastern part of the country were also encouraged to settle.

Methods of promotion varied but often used inflated language to entice immigrants to the Northwest and plains. Some brochures simply painted overly rosy pictures of what life in the Northwest was like, a mild exaggeration of truth.

Others outright lied to prospective settlers, making absurd claims. Upon arrival at their new homes, many settlers became dismayed when the reality of the landscape contrasted greatly with the railroad promoters' claims of paradise. While some surely fled, many ultimately stayed. By the turn of the century, thousands of European immigrants had settled in the Northwest and plains.

The immigrant cars were raw, basic transportation designed for high capacity with little consideration for comfort. They offered only the most spartan accommodations. The sleeping berths were small and unupholstered. Immigrant travelers were expected to provide their own bedding. The Northern Pacific would sell bedding to those without. Pillows cost twenty-five cents and mattresses and blankets were available for seventy-five cents apiece.

First- and second-class passenger trains received exemplary handling across the railroad, progressing from station to station according to published schedules. Immigrant trains made slow plodding progress across the West. Such trains did not receive high priority from railroad dispatchers, and an immigrant might wait for hours on a desolate siding, far from humanity and comfort, while express trains and freights roared past.

Few images exist of these trains. The railroad, which was quick to document much of its operation in drawings and photographs, quietly ignored the immigrant trains. Its chief photographer, F. Jay Haynes, who meticulously documented the Northern Pacific, seems to have overlooked them. Perhaps it was felt that immigrant trains were too insignificant to deserve a place in the annals of railroading. Perhaps no one believed that these trains were worth the price of film. Or maybe the railroad was embarrassed by the pitiful quality of the immigrant accommodations. The immigrants themselves, and their settlement, were highly valued by the railroad and were duly recorded by Haynes and others on film.

While there is little photographic documentation of the immigrant trains, they were undoubtedly successful. All along the Northern Pacific, through Minnesota and the Dakota and Montana territories, towns sprang up and flourished. Even today, more than one hundred years later, the vast majority of the population of Montana and North Dakota can still be found along the route of the Northern Pacific.

Northern Pacific provided special trains to transport immigrating families from the East to their prospective homesteads. The railroad invested in its future by allowing poor settlers and their livestock to ride free of charge. However, the accommodations offered to immigrants reflected the price exacted. While the railroad claimed in its advertisements that there were few differences between the cars provided to immigrant travelers and the first-class sleepers of wealthy patrons, in reality the immigrant cars stood in stark contrast to Northern Pacific's luxury Pullman Palace Cars. True, both operated on steel wheels on the same rails, and were hauled by Northern Pacific's steam locomotives, but the similarities ended with those basic elements.

ABOVE: Immigrant trains like this one, circa 1869, were often crowded, dirty, and unpleasant. They were, however, integral to the growth of the West. OPPOSITE: The Northern Pacific facilitated settling much of the northern plains and Pacific Northwest.

baron Jay Gould. When Villard realized that he should either abandon his transcontinental crusade or acquire the Northern Pacific, Villard chose the more difficult route. He decided to purchase controlling interest in the Northern Pacific. This was risky indeed; the Northern Pacific had already brought one financial giant to ruin, and in more than fifteen years had offered more promises of glory than any real profits. But the Northern Pacific was, to many, the hope of prosperity in the Pacific Northwest. The thought of a completed Northern Pacific line was euphoric: if it could just be completed, all the problems of the region would be solved.

Nothing of this magnitude comes easily, and even for the shrewd Henry Villard, acquiring the Northern Pacific proved a challenge. He did not have the cash reserves to acquire the control he needed. Furthermore, if he announced his plans in an effort to raise funds, he would drive up the price of Northern

Pacific stock, thus finding himself in an expensive bidding war for control of the property. His solution was ingenious. Relying on his solid business reputation, he circulated information to select investors that he was forming a "blind pool" that would be used to make an undisclosed purchase. The scheme proved very successful, and Villard received more than enough capital to take control of Northern Pacific.

Soon after he obtained control, Villard realized that it would be foolish not to complete the projected mainline through the Cascades. So despite concerns about Portland, he agreed to finish the railroad as planned. But he also fulfilled his promise to give Portland its transcontinental link by connecting the Northern Pacific with his Oregon Railway & Navigation line at Pasco. Under Villard's control, the Northern Pacific, which had been making slow progress building across the plains, was rushed to completion. Nearly twenty years in the making, the Northern

OPPOSITE: *A construction crew poses with a locomotive at the Green River on the west slope of the Cascades in 1885.*

LEFT: *Gold Creek, located east of Missoula, in the Montana Territory, was the site of the well-orchestrated "Last Spike" ceremony on September 8, 1883, marking the completion of Henry Villard's Northern Pacific.*

Pacific was finally finished with a great ceremony at Gold Creek, in the Montana Territory, on September 8, 1883.

Villard's empire began to unravel as quickly as he had put it together. Shortly after the ceremonies commemorating the completion of the Northern Pacific, Villard was on the road to ruin. Part of his problem stemmed from the excessive cost of building the Northern Pacific. He had spent some fourteen million dollars more than anticipated. In early 1884, his financing collapsed and he lost control of both the Oregon Railway & Navigation Company and Northern Pacific. Yet just three years after this disaster, Villard would return to the Northern Pacific and remain there until the Panic of 1893. Then, another ambitious empire builder would take the reins of the Northern Pacific, along with other regional railroads, and change the way railroading in the Northwest was done. This man was James Jerome Hill.

JAMES J. HILL

A man of legendary stature, James Jerome Hill loomed high above most of his contemporaries. With high integrity, a short temper, and an unyielding work ethic, he played a crucial role in railroad building in the northern plains and Pacific Northwest. Known to many simply as the Empire Builder, Hill had a reputation as a fierce businessman and he stirred the ire of many living in the Northwest. He was a maverick and a formidable opponent, and he viewed railroading with great seriousness. He was born with next to nothing and thrived through his own handiwork and shrewd thinking. He overcame many hardships, including

blindness in one eye (the result of a childhood fishing accident), and succeeded in nearly every business he entered. He labored hard in pursuit of his dreams, occasionally took daring chances, and was richly rewarded for his efforts. When he died he had accumulated more than fifty million dollars and established one of the strongest, most powerful, and ultimately most enduring railroad networks in North America. His lines spanned more than half a continent and dominated several regions of the country, including the Pacific Northwest.

He was born in Ontario, Canada, in 1838, but spent most of his life in Minnesota's Twin Cities, where he settled before he was twenty. One of his first successful business ventures was the Red River Transportation Company, a steamship company based in St. Paul. Within a short time, he controlled shipping in the Red River Valley. He entered the railroad business in 1873, at a time when many railroads were failing. The Panic of 1873 had scared many railroad investors, and railroad schemes across the country had stalled for want of funds and skilled leadership. Hill saw a great opportunity in the failure of a local railroad, the floundering St. Paul & Pacific. With the help of three partners (Norman Wittson, George Stephen, and Donald Smith) he bought control and renamed it the St. Paul, Minneapolis & Winnipeg. He extended the property to Winnipeg, Manitoba, and linked it with the Canadian Pacific, another line in which he had an interest.

Two Canadian Pacific principals (Stephen and Smith) were Hill's partners, and the excursion into Canada seemed lucrative. But when Canadian Pacific took to building lines that competed with his own, Hill decided to build his own line clear across the plains and over the mountains to the Pacific Coast. In its infancy, Hill's northern transcontinental project was decried as folly: Northern Pacific was fifteen years in the making and not yet close to completing its northern transcontinental route.

Regardless of what less daring minds thought, Hill was determined to build his railroad to the Pacific, even if he had to do it without massive federal land grants. The little land grant money he had was left over from the St. Paul, Minneapolis & Winnipeg venture; most of his funding had to be raised privately.

Hill built slowly and surely across what is now North Dakota. There was no racing against the time limits established in land grant deadlines. Railroads like the Northern Pacific did not enjoy such a luxury. They had to throw down a main-line of shoddy quality, with no time or money left over to build

LEFT: Before railroad lines to Portland were completed, Oregon was a remote part of the nation. Several railroads built lines toward Portland during the late 1880s. The coming of the railroad ushered in a new era of prosperity for the Pacific Northwest.

ABOVE: *A Great Northern passenger train led by 4-6-2 Pacific-type locomotive No. 1459 was captured on film at Seattle, Washington, by well-known Western railroad photographer Charles Clegg.*

necessary feeder lines. From the beginning, Hill built solid lines. Unlike those of his competitors, his lines would not need complete reconstruction shortly after completion. As he moved westward, his network of branch lines fed his transcontinental trunk with adequate traffic to keep his railroad, now named Great Northern, healthy and viable. When the Great Northern reached the coast in 1893, the railroad was not heavily dependent on fickle transcontinental traffic, giving Hill an additional competitive advantage. When the worst financial downturn in twenty years struck—the Panic of 1893—bankruptcy claimed

many lines, including the Northern Pacific. Hill was in an excellent position to take advantage of the situation.

With the help of the great financier J. P. Morgan, Hill seized control of Northern Pacific, Great Northern's primary competition. And while he was unable to merge Northern Pacific with Great Northern, together the two lines dominated traffic moving to and from the Pacific Northwest. Hill went on to acquire the profitable Chicago, Burlington & Quincy—known simply as the "Q"—a route that nicely complemented Great Northern's and Northern Pacific's. It gave both lines access to Chicago, the

LEFT: *The* William Crooks, *built in 1861 by the New Jersey Locomotive & Machine Company, was the first locomotive to operate on Great Northern's predecessor, Minnesota & Pacific.*

BELOW: *James J. Hill built his Great Northern from the Twin Cities to Seattle without the assistance of massive federal grants.*

nation's largest railroad hub, and allowed Hill access to other crucial gateways like St. Louis, Missouri; Omaha, Nebraska; and Denver, Colorado. The three railroads, together known as the Hill Lines, represented one of the most powerful systems in the United States. But when Hill took control of the Burlington, he set off a war with E. H. Harriman, who controlled the powerful Union Pacific (and later also the Southern Pacific). For the rest of their lives Hill and Harriman would vie for superiority in the Northwest, one of the last great railroad feuds, and among the most vicious and well publicized of the early twentieth century.

Harriman himself had been planning to take control of the Q when Hill and Morgan stole it from under his nose. Later, Harriman would come close to wresting Northern Pacific away from Hill. They would continue to fight, building new lines into each other's territory and slashing rates. In Oregon, armed men accompanied work gangs, as the two rivals built competing lines on opposite banks of the Deschutes River. Hill had hoped to build a line to San Francisco, and Harriman was doing his damnedest to keep him out. Even after both men had passed from the scene, their companies continued to fight.

class service between the Twin Cities and Seattle, Washington, with a section to Portland, Oregon. The ride aboard the luxurious *North Coast Limited*—across the great plains of the Dakotas, through the scenic river canyons of Montana, and over the Continental Divide and the rugged Cascade Mountains of Washington—must have given its well-to-do patrons a great sense of satisfaction. The railroad had conquered the wilds of the Northwest and provided service in the grandest style. A generation earlier, travelers had had to risk life and limb, face unknown perils, and spend months crossing the wilderness on foot or in an ox-drawn wagon to reach Portland or Seattle. In a triumph of ingenuity, man had brought the Northwest—that wildest of places—into submission, and now traveled fearlessly across its once prohibitive, vast terrain to view its scenic splendor in comfort.

Northern Pacific had been providing through passenger service on its routes since its completion, but the *North Coast Limited*'s premier service was an improvement. Patrons could enjoy the new train's deluxe accommodations and experience its exceptional amenities: electric lights and fans—at a time when few households had such wonders. This train offered more than raw transportation, it offered style and class.

Perhaps the *North Coast Limited*'s most famous feature—one that would soon become common on luxury trains throughout America—was its grand, open-platform observation cars. The *North Coast* was the one of the first trains to feature these icons of early-twentieth-century passenger travel. Northern Pacific took advantage of these novelties, picturing them in advertising and on train schedules. The observation car was strictly for recreation; the railroad opened the observation car to the train's passengers and enticed them to partake of its luxuries. The observation car featured a library containing nearly two hundred titles and the latest popular magazines; on the end of the car a 6-foot-six-inch-by-9-foot (2m × 2.7m) open observation platform enabled passengers to soak up the splendors of the Northwest. Perhaps an even greater attribute of the observation platform was the photo opportunities. How many great celebrities posed with the Oriental yin and yang—Northern Pacific's herald, commonly referred to as the monad—on the observation drumhead? Babe Ruth and Queen Marie of Romania were among the many.

Noted railroad author Lucius Beebe commented on one of the train's most civilized accommodations: "Among the identifying

ABOVE: *Passengers aboard Northern Pacific's* North Coast Limited *were assured of comfort on their way west. Long before electric lighting was a household convenience, NP provided it on its flagship train.*

THE NORTH COAST LIMITED

The Pacific Northwest was considered the epitome of the American frontier—the most wild, untamed place in the continental United States. Train and stage robbers, hostile Native Americans, raging winter storms, and an immense wilderness earned the region its reputation. The Northern Pacific Railroad was the entity that would open up the Pacific Northwest to settlement, and the completion of the Northern Pacific brought a much-hoped-for prosperity to the region.

By the time Northern Pacific inaugurated its most famous train, the *North Coast Limited*, on April 29, 1900, the legendary status of the Northwest was already embedded in the American consciousness. But the Northwest had been, in essence, domesticated. At first a seasonal train, the *North Coast* provided first-

EVERY LUXURY ∮ TRAVEL IS FOUND ON THE "NORTH COAST LIMITED". ITS OBSERVATION CAR IS A REVELATION OF BEAUTY—EXCEPTIONALLY ATTRACTIVE TO WOMEN TRAVELERS. LIBRARY; HOT AND COLD BATHS; BUFFET AND OTHER CONVENIENCES. GO WEST VIA **NORTHERN PACIFIC RAILWAY** YELLOWSTONE NATIONAL PARK *en route*

A.M. CLELAND, GENERAL PASSENGER AGENT, ST. PAUL, MINN.
SEND SIX CENTS EACH FOR "WONDERLAND 1906" AND "EASTWARD THROUGH THE STORIED NORTHWEST."

LEFT: *Northern Pacific's* North Coast Limited *was one of the first trains to offer an open-platform observation car. This luxury was heavily advertised to entice Eastern travelers to choose Northern Pacific.*

OPPOSITE: *The elegant Victorian furnishings of the* North Coast Limited *display the luxury for which the train was known.*

hallmarks of a train of pedigree in the great years of luxury travel [and] one of the foremost status symbols was, of course, the barber shop. . . " Like a few other luxury trains of the day, the *North Coast Limited* featured a barber shop, the first in Pacific Northwest railroading. The shop was normally found in the forward, combination baggage-buffet car. The barber was a nimble virtuoso skilled in the use of scissors and the straight razor to avoid cutting his paying patrons when working while riding over rough track.

While the railroad originally intended the *North Coast Limited* to be a seasonal daily service, its great popularity led Northern Pacific to place it on a year-round daily schedule in the 1902 season. To accomplish this, ten sets of the most elegant wooden heavyweight cars dedicated to the service were purchased from Pullman. Each train had eight cars, including the observation car, and the cost for this equipment in 1900 was a staggering $800,000. Among the equipment on the *North Coast* were Palace Cars, elegant sleeping cars that converted to luxury passenger cars in daylight hours, the very zenith of wooden passenger-car construction. One of the *North Coast*'s typical observation cars, also described as a library-lounge-buffet car, featured interior decoration in the Victorian tradition—highly polished walnut with deep blue velvet upholstery and matching cushioned wicker chairs. A clerestory roof with arched windows augmented the light entering the car from the large side and end windows. In his book *The Trains We Rode*, Lucius Beebe romantically described a *North Coast* observation car in glowing superlatives: "Its brocaded velvet valances and tulip-shaded electroliers lent it a beauty remarkable in a period of splendid Palace Cars from Pullman." The wonderful Pullmans were supplemented by cars manufactured by Barney & Smith, many of which featured unusual and distinct interiors; one such observation car was decorated with elaborate Old English decor.

For much of its long life the *North Coast Limited* carried the numbers 1 and 2. No. 1 was westbound; No. 2, eastbound. Its original schedule found the train zipping between St. Paul, Minnesota, and Puget Sound in under sixty-three hours. Officials of the railroad took great pride in their premier train, regularly upgrading the equipment with the latest features. To pull the train, only the finest, fastest locomotives were employed. Following the turn of the century, great strides were being made in locomotive development, so every few years the *North Coast Limited* found itself with larger, more powerful, engines. In 1900

Northern Pacific's premier passenger engines were Schenectady-built Ten-Wheelers featuring three pairs of very large—73 inch (185cm)—driving wheels. By 1909, the Pacific-type locomotive, with the 4-6-2 wheel arrangement (a set of wheels behind the firebox allowed for a larger firebox and thus more power), had replaced the Ten-Wheelers on choice runs. And by the mid-1920s the Pacific had given way to the still larger and more powerful Baldwin-built Northern type. Big locomotives with 4-8-4 wheel arrangements, the Northern type ruled the fast passenger runs in the Pacific Northwest until the diesel electric took over following World War II.

Northern Pacific's majestic locomotives were the wonder of every child that saw them race by. Adults, too, were awed and encouraged by the sight and sound of these great engines. Author Edward W. Nolan notes that well-known twentieth-century composer Arthur Honegger was on board the inaugural *North Coast Limited* in 1900. The ride evidently inspired Honegger to create his best-known work, the symphonic poem *Pacific 231*. Indeed, the locomotive pictured leading that first *North Coast* bore the number "231." Ironically, this proud locomotive, with its polished wooden cow-catcher pilot, high-mounted headlight, and gleaming boiler was not a Pacific type, but one of Northern Pacific's Ten-Wheelers. Perhaps Honegger was referring to the ocean rather than the locomotive.

Pacific Northwest matched its locomotive improvements with equivalent upgrades of its passenger cars. The *North Coast Limited* experienced substantive revampings in 1909, and again in 1930. A Northern Pacific advertisement from the 1920s proclaimed the splendid fittings found aboard its great train.

> *Every sleeping car in the North Coast Limited is "brand new"—just built by the Pullman Company—embodying the very latest designs, improvements, refinements and comforts. Particular attention has been given to the interior decorations and colors, which will appeal to men and women travelers alike. The new steel cars of the ten-section, two-compartment and drawing room type, are finished in Circassian walnut, both in the body of the car and in the compartment and drawing-rooms. The upholstering is blue plush with rich carpets and window shades in harmony. The women's dressing rooms in these cars are of large size with a wide mirror across one end and convenient dressing tables and chairs.*

Riding the trains of the 1930s, passengers were treated to the standard of luxury they had become accustomed to in the latest styles. The interior decoration of the new consist featured rose, green, and light brown interiors, amenities such as radio for entertainment, and both baths and showers for men and women. For a safer, smoother ride, the cars were equipped with Timken roller bearings—a revolutionary technology that used a system of bearings to hold the wheel-axle in place, reducing the chances of a dreaded "hot box." Hot boxes were dangerous flaws caused by excessive friction between the axle and journal; they could result in delays, or worse, in grisly derailments, when the friction caused the journal to melt while the train was moving at speed.

The *North Coast* was only one of Northern Pacific's stylish trains. Always looking to promote its name trains, a 1912 Northern Pacific advertisement touted the virtues of both the *North Coast Limited* and its sister trains, the *Northern Pacific Express* and the *Puget Sound Limited*, "Electric-lighted service of the highest order and the latest type, with dining car meals that are world-famous identifying 'Northern Pacific' as the 'Route of the Great BIG Baked Potato': the line with its own bakery and butcher shop and a poultry farm and dairy farm." Other elegant posters portrayed romantic images of the trains against fantastic backdrops of Western scenery.

Following World War II the *North Coast Limited* underwent a spectacular metamorphosis. The railroad made a serious commitment to the train by taking a leap into the streamlined age. In 1946 the railroad spent ten million dollars and ordered all new streamlined consists, including nearly eighty passenger cars from Pullman and new diesel-electric locomotives from Electro-Motive. The six streamlined consists proved popular with riders.

In 1952 Northern Pacific hired Raymond Loewy, the renowned industrial designer, to style the *North Coast Limited*. Loewy had inspired streamlined railroad design in the 1930s with such famous trains as the Pennsylvania's GG1 electric locomotive. His celebrated designs combined aesthetics and functionality. Loewy designed an attractive two-tone green paint scheme to adorn the *North Coast Limited*'s exterior, incorporating the Northern Pacific's Oriental monad. The interior decoration featured tasteful Art Deco styling of the period, using distinctive pastel colors that lent an air of class and style. The diner's interior decoration featured copper tones that Loewy felt represented the Pacific Northwest. In 1953, *Railway Age* described the diner's

BELOW: *Initially the* **North Coast Limited** *was only operated seasonally. However, the popularity of the train soon mandated year-round service.*

decor: "Sideways walls have a dull luster finish that gives the illusion of burnished copper and which reflects the copper tones of the bulkhead plaques and the copper hued carpeting. The windows are draped in a specially designed fabric of semigeometric slate blue and copper motifs. Overhead lighting is recessed and is directed on each table by round fixtures in one area and rectangular fixtures in another to vary the ceiling treatment."

In conjunction with the Loewy restyling, Northern Pacific tightened the *North Coast Limited*'s schedule to just 46½ hours between Chicago and Seattle.

In 1954 Northern Pacific implemented another dramatic improvement to its *North Coast Limited*; it purchased twenty-two Budd-built Vista Domes. Already popular on other Western railroads, Vista Domes allowed passengers an elevated, panoramic view of passing horizons.

Northern Pacific maintained the *North Coast Limited* throughout the 1960s, when many other railroads allowed their premier trains to deteriorate. It was a popular, well patronized train up until nearly the end of its life. While name trains such as Southern Pacific's *Sunset Limited* became austere shadows of their former glory, the *North Coast* remained a classy, luxury train. It became known as the "oldest named train in the west" as other railroads altered the names of the great limiteds. The *North Coast Limited* outlived the Northern Pacific, if by just a few months. In 1970 Northern Pacific and the other Hill Lines—Great Northern; Chicago, Burlington & Quincy; and Spokane, Portland & Seattle—were merged together to form the Burlington Northern, which was then the largest railroad in the United States.

The *North Coast* succumbed in May 1971, when federally sponsored Amtrak assumed most intercity passenger operations. During the 1970s, Amtrak operated a train called the *North Coast Hiawatha* on the route of the Northern Pacific's great limited, but the *Hiawatha* paled in comparison. In 1979 it was unceremoniously killed in a round of budget cuts. In the mid-1990s a semblance of the *North Coast* was revived when several privately operated luxury trains offered "cruise train" tours across Montana on a portion of the old Northern Pacific. Nevertheless, the halcyon days of the reign of the *North Coast Limited's* are best remembered in photographs and memorabilia.

CHAPTER FIVE

SNOW WARS

❧

OPPOSITE: *Central Pacific Bucker Plow No. 4 pauses for its portrait at Blue Canyon. To clear its tracks of heavy snow, the Central Pacific would use as many as eight locomotives to shove a Bucker Plow through the drifts.*

SNOW PLOWS

Railroading in the West produced a whole new breed of railroader and railroad equipment. The reason is simple: Western railroads had to overcome more extreme natural obstacles than those encountered by their Eastern counterparts. One such obstacle was the scarcity of necessary commodities, such as wood and coal for fuel, and water for locomotive boilers. Fuel and water are found in great abundance in the East but are extremely scarce or nonexistent in much of the West. The cost of transporting fuel and water was a serious consideration when planning operations. In the Western deserts, even the small amount of water available was too poor in quality to be used in engine boilers.

The Western mountains were also formidable obstacles to engineers. The Sierra, the Rockies, and the Cascades presented a much greater challenge to railroad builders than the Eastern Appalachians. Mountain routes in the West required fantastic construction using tunnels, tall trestles, sharp curves, loops, and occasionally even switchbacks. In a switchback the tracks would double back to gain elevation, forcing ascending trains to back up. In places, railroads cut out of rock clung to mountain sides. Railroad engineers put railroads in places where a previous generation had not dared even to walk!

In the East it was unusual to find long stretches of mainline railroad with grades steeper than 2 percent, while in the West railroads often built their lines on even steeper grades. Once completed, the Northern Pacific featured several long grades of

2.2 percent over Montana's Mullen Pass, Bozeman Pass, and Homestake Pass, and Washington's Stampede Pass. These grades were considered far superior to those of the temporary lines that the railroad employed in its infancy. The ruling eastbound grade on the Central Pacific in the Sierra was 2.4 percent. The Santa Fe employed several long stretches of 3 percent on its Raton and Glorieta Pass crossings in New Mexico, on its twisting winding line to Phoenix, and on its route of Cajon Pass in southern California. The Oregon & California (later, the Southern Pacific line to Portland from California) employed many miles of line in excess of 3 percent in the Siskiyou Mountains of southern Oregon. The railroads that crossed the Rockies in Colorado and northern New Mexico featured some of North America's most incredible track work. Steep, winding tracks often clung precariously to the sides of high cliffs, thousands of feet above river gorges. The Denver & Rio Grande narrow gauge had long stretches of winding 4-percent grade, most notable on its spectacular eastbound climb to the 10,000-foot-high (3,048m) Cumbres Pass. Denver, South Park & Pacific's three-foot-gauge (91cm) line similarly crawled up a sinuous 4 percent to its legendary Alpine tunnel more than 11,000 feet (3,353m) above sea level. But perhaps the most incredible line ever constructed was David Moffat's standard-gauge Denver & Salt Lake line, known as the Giant's Ladder, which ascended the Front Range of the Rockies east of Denver on an intense 4-percent line with many switchbacks. It crossed the Continental Divide at Rollins Pass, a dizzying 11,680 (3,560m) feet above sea level. Yet, steep grades, switchbacks, tunnels, and high altitudes paled in comparison to the one natural phenomenon that caused railroaders the greatest grief—snow!

On Donner, on Rollins, on Stampede, and on Stevens the enemy of railroaders was indeed snow—the most formidable obstacle in the West. Its fickle behavior, unpredictable volume, and sheer mass brought havoc to Western rails not conceivable in the East. The snowfall potential on Western mountain passes was enormous. Easterners might be alarmed by a storm that brought six to eight inches (15–20cm) of snow; Westerners might have to cope with storms that dumped six to eight feet (183–244cm) of snow. And while just one such storm might be devastating, storm after storm could bring catastrophic results. The snow pack could exceed twenty feet (6m), and blowing, drifting snow could exceed thirty feet (9m).

This huge amount of snow paralyzed operations, stranded trains, and shut down crucial railroad lines for days and weeks at a time. Whole trains were swept off the tracks by avalanches. In some cases, snow buried a railroad for an entire season.

At high elevations, snow can start as early as August and might still be falling the following June. In some places it never completely melts, but clings to mountaintops in small glaciers. Not all winters are equal. Many years pass without significant snowfall; other years bring a continuing procession of winter storms. The railroads had to cope with even the very worst weather. Sometimes they triumphed; other times, despite gallant efforts, they were beaten. High mountain passes get the worst snow, but the plains are also susceptible to tremendous snowfalls. Here, without trees or other natural barriers to impede its progress, the wind blows the snow into fantastic drifts that become barriers across frozen railroad tracks.

Early in their conquest, the builders of Western railroads were confronted with the harsh realities of winter. One of the snowiest places in the West is Donner Pass—the granddaddy of all Western railroad grades. Yet, when the great surveyor and railroad promoter Theodore Judah inspected Donner, very little snow covered the ground. When he was exploring the route for his Pacific Railroad, the Sierra was experiencing one of its driest winters on record. He estimated snowfall at the summit would rarely exceed a depth of thirteen feet (4m). Judah believed that while snow would hamper operations, the problem could be solved by simply running trains back and forth to keep snow from accumulating on the tracks. Judah could not have imagined his railroad at Norden buried under more than twenty feet (6m) of wet Sierra snow. He had completely miscalculated the snowfall potential on Donner Pass, one of his few great flaws as a surveyor, and one for which his successors would have to compensate.

In a wet winter, Pacific storms hit California bringing heavy rain to the coast. As the storms reach the Sierra they dump tremendous amounts of snow at high elevations. The snow line varies greatly depending on the temperature. A tropical storm may result in rain even at the highest levels, while a cold Alaskan storm can bring snow down to an elevation of only one thousand feet (305m) above sea level. Normally, the snow line hovers around five thousand feet (1,524m) above sea level.

The winter of 1866 was especially cruel, bringing more than forty feet of snow. It was during that memorable season that Charlie Crocker's forces were desperately struggling to push the Central Pacific over the mountains. Every day counted, since they were competing with the Union Pacific, vying for territory in the race to complete the first transcontinental railroad. In his book *Snowplow: Clearing Mountain Rails*, author Gerald Best describes Crocker's efforts.

> *An army of snow shovelers including most of the grading force was required to keep the ground clear. So heavy was the December 1866 snowfall that most of the available work force removed snow as grading proceeded with a small gang of men. At one time during that winter, the snowfall was so great that the only work which could be done was that of building the 1,650-foot tunnel through the mountain at Donner Summit. Men working within the tunnel's bore could continue without interruption. To dispose of the rock, snow galleries were excavated through the mountainous drifts, the rock being brought out and dumped into hollows in the snow at the ends of the galleries.*

Demonstrating the need for continued eastward progress, Best relates Crocker's desperate attempts to keep building, when progress at the summit had become nearly stalled.

> *…fitting huge logs together to make sleds, [Crocker] used oxen to haul rails, locomotives, cars and track supplies to build forty miles of railroad in the valley of the Truckee River east of Truckee [California] where the snow presented no great difficulty.*

If just building the railroad in these conditions took such effort, then regular operations would prove a real nightmare. To relieve some of the problems caused by the great snowfall on Donner, Crocker's forces built roughly forty miles (64km) of wooden snowsheds over the tracks where the railroad encountered the heaviest snowfall, primarily near the summit between Emigrant Gap and Andover, California. These snowsheds, some of the most extensive ever built, created miles of tunnel-like conditions that came to be known colloquially as "railroading in a barn."

Snowsheds solved part of the problem, but they could not be constructed along the entire line. The snowfall potential in Nevada, and along the Union Pacific line in what are today Wyoming and Nebraska, also presented operating nightmares. To handle the relatively light demands of winter railroading in the

heavily ballasted, weighing some twelve tons (11t). Later the weight was increased to nearly twenty tons (18t). Central Pacific built ten Bucker Plows and used them to keep the tracks over Donner clear of snow for many years. In extremely harsh weather eight locomotives might be used behind the wedge as it careened through drifting snow. The plows frequently became stuck. When they did they were extricated the old-fashioned way, by man and shovel. The railroad kept hundreds of men employed shoveling snow in the High Sierra in the winter.

The railroad was not a novelty, it was the lifeline between California and the rest of the nation. If the railroad shut down because of snow and could not run its trains, then California was cut off. Furthermore, if the railroad did not run trains, it made no money. So management did whatever was necessary to keep the tracks clear at all times of year.

Wild Ride on a Plow

Although necessary, snow fighting was very dangerous business. In *Snow Plow*, Gerald Best reprints an article from the Truckee *Republican*, written in January 1880 by the paper's editor and columnist, C. F. McGlashan after a harrowing ride aboard a Central Pacific plow train on Donner Pass.

East, railroads equipped their locomotives with broad plows to keep the tracks clear. This solution was not entirely practical in the West, where drifting snow often exceeded the height of the average steam locomotive.

To combat the severe snow, Central Pacific forces had to develop more creative means of clearing it from the tracks. The railroad's Sacramento shops invented a clever device called a Bucker Plow. This was essentially a large wedge-like wooden box riding on two sets of flange wheels. The front of the wedge drooped down to track level and was fitted with an adjustable iron blade. The rear of the wedge was higher than the locomotive. Midway up the wedge another wedge was fitted to send snow to the sides. The plow had no power of its own and was designed to be pushed along by one or more locomotives.

The Bucker Plow proved reasonably successful, although plowing through deep drifts was hazardous business. To prevent derailments as the trains charged through snow, plows were

The gale increased until it became a hurricane. Early in the day it became evident that a new and hitherto unheard of danger threatened the Central Pacific. It was a danger that caused the bravest men to turn pale. The snowsheds showed indications of falling....Before the storm of Friday, they trembled and tottered and each instant threatened to fall. The westbound lightning express plunged into a slide near Yuba Pass and seriously injured George Hamilton, the engineer, and his fireman.

Soon after noon, 100 feet of corrugated iron shed blew down near the same place and freight train No. 6 went crashing into the ruins. The collision caused another large section of shedding to fall, and the doomed train was buried beneath a mass of broken timbers and deep piled drifts. Three men were completely hidden from sight, but providentially suffered no serious injury. Buckley's snowplow ran to the wreck with a full crew of workmen, and by great exertion succeeded in drawing the rear cars of No. 6 back to Cisco. Meanwhile 500 feet of snowsheds fell between that point

and Emigrant Gap. The snow drifted heavily through the openings in the sheds, and accumulated so rapidly that Buckley's train could not return to the summit. It was literally imprisoned at Cisco.

A storm on the Sierra means toil and danger to hundreds of poor fellows. The engineers and firemen, the conductors and brakemen, the operators, train dispatchers, foremen and superintendents all have multiplied toil and exposure. The warfare between these men and the elements is worthy of being better understood. It is a warfare wherein brain and muscle are arrayed against cold, darkness and avalanches, against death in a thousand forms.

William Hackett, a brakeman on No. 6, Friday morning was knocked off the car and falling beneath the wheels was crushed and killed....

At tunnel No. 9 two miles east of the summit, a watchman found it impossible to pass the huge drifts, and attempting to turn back found that a snowslide had blocked the way. In utter despair he kindled a fire in the tunnel and sat down to wait until relief came. It was extremely cold.

...Orders came from Supt. Pratt for a second plow to run to the summit. Train Dispatcher W.R. Watson who was on duty throughout the entire storm immediately ordered six engines to be attached to Plow No. 5. In order to meet any emergency, two crews were placed on the plow, Joe Coburn's and Henry Wooden's. Fred Graham, M. Norton, George Hamilton and William Dolan composed these crews. Believing that he who writes the description of a battle must catch the inspiration on the battle field, the Republican editor was in this plow. A night storm on the Sierra is a grand spectacle. The fury and power of the winds, the blinding snowdust, the piercing cold, the bleak, awe-inspiring mountains, the preternatural gloom, the ghostly, ice clad forests, the dark, shadowy gorges and the dreadful loneliness and helplessness of the situation are calculated to awaken the sublimest emotions.

Of late years no headlights are placed on the plows. From the moment the hoarse whistles indicate the start, all in front of the plow is in profound darkness. There is no limit to the speed of a snowplow train, and when flying in the teeth of a hurricane,

ABOVE: *This drawing by Charles Graham depicts a "wedge" plow at work clearing snow from the northern plains.*

Snow Wars

When the momentum was finally overcome it was necessary for the engines to back down to the woodpile. A snowplow cannot be backed without being thrown off the track, for the loose snow gets under the apron and lifts the ponderous plow bodily from the rails. Accordingly, the plow was uncoupled and left standing while the engines went back to the sheds. In due time they were supplied with fuel and the whistles sounded "off brakes."

The darkness was so intense that none of the engineers, except the head one, knew that the plow had been detached. As a result five of the engines started out of the shed at full speed. While the engines were wooding up, the two crews came down from the top platform and were standing inside the plow. After the engines had got under way, these men discovered that there was some misunderstanding, and that a frightful collision would occur when the six engines struck the plow. With a rush for the door at the rear of the snowplow, each one endeavored to jump out into the snow by the side of the track. The banks thrown up by the plow were from four to six feet in height and one could not spring upon them from the door. It was necessary to climb up on the iron ladder on the rear of the plow and to spring therefrom. One by one the six men in the car climbed the ladder and escaped. Graham climbed on the plow and sitting astride the safety rope braced himself to withstand the shock.

The head engineers had screamed for "down brakes" but the flying engines on the icy rails had no power to check the speed. Wooden was the last man out, and just as the collision came he partly sprang and was partly hurled out into the snow. The last man did we say? No! The Republican editor was just behind Wooden and had just grasped the top round of the ladder as the engines struck. Couplings of the head engine were crushed into fragments. The hind end of the snowplow was shivered as if by a stroke of lightning, and the plow was dashed ahead as if suddenly shot from a cannon. Every engine felt the heavy shock and the wheels of each were instantly reversed.

Knocked from the ladder, the Republican man struck some portion of the forward engine. In a twinkling he was rolled and crumpled in all conceivable shapes between the engines and the clean shaven snow wall left by the plow. Perfectly conscious, he was nevertheless as helpless as a straw in a threshing machine. Indeed, the principal thought at such a moment is a wonderful appreciation of the majestic power of a

ABOVE: *In the early days of the Central Pacific, a few miles west of Auburn, California, in the Sierra foothills, a train passes through Bloomer Cut—a narrow passage in the rocks that took weeks of blasting with black powder to clear.*

it is impossible to face the darting snow granules, which cut and sting the eyes like needlepoints. Up over the mold-boards of the plow come huge masses of snow which sometimes seem ready to bury one.

It is a true saying that one-half the world does not know what the other half is doing, and few people have any conception of the constant perils of these railroaders. As an example, perhaps the following is not amiss. It was intended that the engines should wood up at Coldstream. Just before the wood-sheds were reached, however, the plowing became so heavy that Coburn pulled the bell-rope for "off brakes." This meant that more power was requisite and the head engine had no sooner sounded the whistle than every engine was working under a full head of steam. The speed was something alarming. It not only cleared the track, but caused the engines to shoot through the long wood shed and far out into the storm and darkness.

LEFT: *In the early days of railroad construction, tunneling was slow, expensive, difficult, and dangerous work.*

ten-wheel, fifty-ton locomotive. Jammed and twisted and whirled and dragged, one has time to wish that a friendly squeeze of the cylinderhead, or a sudden clash of the walking beam would end the agony, rather than that the cruel wheels should close the scene.

But there is a constant tendency downward, and finally a sudden drop under the wheels. The darkness of a stormy night is absolute blackness under a train of moving engines. There is not a ray of light. No light could have aided in a complete realization of the situation. Every muscle quivers as it touches the whirling, grinding wheels. One is dragged along by their very contact, yet not fast enough to escape being overtaken by the truck-wheels and drivers of the next locomotive. One thinks that death is delayed but one instant and wonders if legs or arms or head will be crushed first. There is no thought of past or future.

Suddenly there is a consciousness that by lying perfectly still and straight there is possible room between the wheels and the snow wall for one's body. Instinctively the wall is hugged. The wheels still graze, graze, graze as they pass. But thank God! They are moving slowly now, and yet more slowly. The train is Stopping! M. Mack is the engineer of the head engine, the 85, and Dan Higgins is fireman. The second is Jim Kelly's engine, the 56, and Ed Dolan is fireman. The 209 is third, C.C. Trott is engineer and C. Weadick fireman. When the train stopped we were lying under this engine. None of these three had pilots. The 58, Lawrence Kearney, engineer and Sam Kennedy, fireman was fourth and had a pilot. This would have crushed us had it passed.

George Spoor's engine, the No. 8, Wm. Weadick, fireman was fifth, and Sam Young's engine, the 200, M. Wallace, fireman, was last. Young's engine was running backward and had a small snowplow on the hind end. This would have made death inevitable. After climbing into Trott's cab it was found that the wheels had torn our over coat and cut off the cape of our hood or sailor's cap. We were quite unhurt. The straw had not been broken in the threshing machine.

The plow is broken but can be pushed to Summit. Had she not been broken, every man on the train probably would have been killed. Orders came to run to Cisco and between Summit and Cisco 800 feet of snowshed lay prostrate. The broken plow could not go, and so the orders were countermanded. Had a snowplow train dashed into the fallen sheds, no man on board would have lived to tell the tale. All Saturday night Standish, with a crew of fifty men worked at the east end of the break. Superintendent Pratt with 400 workmen worked on the west end. By nine o'clock Sunday morning the road was open. The snowstorm had cleared away.

Alpine Crossing

The Central Pacific crossed Donner at seven thousand feet (2,134m) above sea level, but this great height was nothing compared to what the narrow-gauge South Park Line in central Colorado had to surmount. At seven thousand feet (2,134m) the South Park was just beginning to climb. This line had multiple summits, but its most famous, most treacherous, and best remembered was the mythic Alpine Tunnel, at a dizzying

altitude of nearly twelve thousand feet (3,658m) above sea level, the highest railroad pass in North America. Between Buena Vista and Gunnison, this twelve-hundred-foot-long (366m) tunnel pierces the Continental Divide on the Saguache Range. Winter takes on a whole new meaning at these high elevations. Building the line took extreme courage, and operating it proved impossible at times.

Raging blizzards, nearly year-long winters, and the constraints of working at very high altitudes conspired to cause the railroad construction problems. The railroad suffered from more than its share of calamity. At one point nearly fifty workers were killed in an explosion meant to loosen rocks. Despite this hardship, the line through the tunnel was finally completed in the summer of 1882.

Some say the Alpine Tunnel was cursed by the Ute Indians, who were displeased by the incursion of white men into Ute territory. The tunnel continually suffered from problems and disasters, lending credence to the myth. The first train through the tunnel, an excursion train filled with railroad dignitaries, was the first victim of the curse. The short train, led by engine No. 11, the *Ouray*, ran out of control on the steep mountain grades. While the engineer was severely injured, no one was killed. Later runs would not fare as well.

The tunnel was often closed by extreme snowfall. Each side of the bore was protected by snowsheds, but intense winter storms and the line's 4-percent grades sometimes prohibited successful snow removal. In the winter the line would remain closed for months at a time. Some years, the railroad management would not attempt to reopen the line at all. The snowfall in winter was prohibitive and winter lasted most of the year. The costs of operating the line exceeded even the most optimistic projected profits, so for seven years, between 1888 and 1895, the railroad sat dormant to through traffic. But when the line finally reopened, the "Alpine Curse" had not lifted. As engineer Dad Martinis brought the first train up through the tunnel (the summit of the line lay in the middle of the bore), he and his crew suffocated to death. Lucius Beebe relates: "[he] was found erect in his seat, his left hand on the air valve, his right on the reverse gear, his beard and clothes ordered." Some say that to this day, Dad Martinis' ethereal spirit haunts the long-abandoned bore. Service through the tunnel was suspended indefinitely in 1910 and never resumed.

Orange Jull and His Competing Plows

Terrible Western winters presented an obvious need for more sophisticated and effective snow removal. Until the mid-1880s, wedge plows and brute force cleared the tracks, but a clever Canadian with the tropical-sounding name of Orange Jull developed a better solution. In 1884 he patented an ingenious device that used a set of rapidly rotating fan-like blades powered by a stationary steam engine to cut into snow and propel it off railroad tracks. Like other snow plows, Jull's Rotary Snowplow was powered by one or more locomotives. Jull was not the first to look for more effective ways to plow snow, but he was the first to do so with success. He assigned his invention to two friends, brothers John S. and Edward Leslie, who modified it with a few inventions of their own. In 1885, the Leslies built their first operating Rotary Snowplow. Actual assembly was completed at the Canadian Pacific Railroad shops near Toronto.

The Leslie Rotary was an instant success. Its whirling blades sliced through deep snow drifts encountering no resistance, clearing tracks quickly and enabling traffic to flow. Soon many railroads were placing orders for the wondrous plow. In 1887 Central Pacific ordered a Rotary to clear snowy Donner Pass. Indeed, Jull had invented the ultimate snow-fighting machine.

Jull felt that he had not been adequately compensated for the great success of his machine and parted ways with the Leslie brothers on less than friendly terms. Not one to sit around moping, Jull was determined to build another, even better snow plow. He started his own company, and in 1889 designed a peculiar-looking steam plow called a Jull Centrifugal Snow Excavator. Instead of a large fan, the new Jull Plow used a giant auger placed on a forty-five-degree angle. The steam engine aboard the plow spun the auger to cut through snow. The plow resembled an oddly-shaped passenger coach with an angled corkscrew on the front.

One of the first tests for the Jull plow was for Union Pacific's Oregon Short Line and Oregon Railway & Navigation

Company, for whom it performed admirably, clearing snow from hundreds of miles of line with few problems. Proud of his new device, eager for rapid sales, and angry over the unrewarding success of the Rotary, Jull launched a media campaign in the railroad trade press proclaiming the advantages of the Jull plow over the Leslie Rotary. With all the vigor of an upstart political candidate lambasting the incumbent, Jull sang high praises for his new machine, dismissing the Rotary as inadequate and incapable. An 1890 advertisement for the Jull Centrifugal Snow Excavator reproduced by Gerald Best reads:

It has done better work than any other snow machine in the market and has never broken down.

In use by the Union Pacific and Pennsylvania Railroads.

It handles the snow but once, and throws it 60 feet or more to either or both sides of the track without reversing, and meets

RIGHT: *E. P. Caldwell's Cyclone Plow attempts to clear Donner Pass. Although impressive-looking, the Cyclone was no match for the Leslie Rotary Snowplow.*

The competition between the Leslie Rotary and Jull's Excavator was fierce. Snow-plow sales were big money—a new steam-powered plow cost more than two thousand dollars. The winter of 1889–90, when Jull's Excavator made its debut, was one of the worst seasons in memory. Particularly hard hit were the Western mountains, and the South Park Line route over the cursed Alpine Pass was no exception. It was there that, in April 1890, snow-plow trials were staged to prove which type plow, the Leslie Rotary or the Jull Excavator, was more adept at removing snow.

Alpine Pass had been closed for an entire season when the railroad—then under the control of the mighty Union Pacific—took delivery of its first steam plow, a three-foot-gauge (91cm) Leslie Rotary, in March 1889. The new plow was constructed under contract by the Cooke Locomotive Works in Paterson, New Jersey. It was the twenty-sixth Leslie Rotary built in a little more than two years, and the third such plow built to narrow-gauge specifications. It was quickly put to work clearing the snow-encrusted rails of the Denver, South Park & Pacific, which was the railroad's proper name at the time. But the legendary line to Gunnison, Colorado, was not the first priority;

with less resistance in excavating snow than any other device.

The Jull Excavator opened the O.R. & N. Co's Railway to traffic after it had been completely blockaded for ten days. During this blockade it did work without difficulty with two locomotives which the Rotary was unable to accomplish with four.

ABOVE: *The most effective tool in snow fighting is the Leslie Rotary Snowplow. An early Leslie Rotary poses with its crew in January of 1890 at the Cascade Bridge, a few miles west of Soda Springs, California, on Donner Pass.*

ABOVE: *Southern Pacific snow-sheds, just west of the summit tunnel on the original alignment over Donner Pass, were built in the 1860s. A slightly lower crossing of Donner was completed in the 1920s.* **OPPOSITE**: *Winter on Donner is a formidable foe. Despite advances in technology, a few Leslie Rotary Plows are still kept handy to keep the tracks clear. In February 1993, Southern Pacific used the rotaries for three days to clear Donner.*

Alpine Pass would have to wait while the snow-plow cleared the line over Boreas Pass to Leadville.

While the Leslie Rotary's snow-fighting abilities proved miraculous—the mighty plow could cut through deep drifts and snow slides without straining and made quick work of lighter snow—its Achilles' heel was rocks and debris. When the rapidly spinning fan of the Rotary dug into snow that contained hard debris, the blades were quickly damaged. Blades were sometimes damaged so severely that the plow would be out of service for days while its fan was repaired. This meant that in areas where avalanches and snow slides had buried the tracks, men still had to work by hand. For this reason, the railroad was eager to test the abilities of the Jull Excavator, which supposedly could handle rocks and debris, and the snow-plow trials were held.

This second Jull Excavator was constructed at the Rogers Locomotive Works, also in Paterson, New Jersey. The two competing plows were brought up to the closed Alpine Pass. Well-known railroad photographer William Henry Jackson was there to record the event with his cumbersome glass-plate camera. The Leslie Rotary, already a South Park workhorse, cleared the line to Romley on the east slope of Alpine Pass a few miles from the east portal of the tunnel. Here the Jull took over. It suffered several derailments, but when it was not on the ground it did a fair job of removing snow from the tracks. After some time, the

Leslie took over and, as usual, performed flawlessly. Again the Jull was put to work—this time clearing some very heavy snow. But the Jull continued to derail. While none of the derailments were serious, crews spent as much time rerailing the plow as they did clearing the tracks. Finally, after three days up on the pass, the Rotary was deemed the winner and proceeded triumphantly to the summit, clearing the right-of-way of very heavy snow. Photographer Jackson exposed some of the most dramatic photographs of his career. The Jull returned to the shops at Denver for modification, but is not known to have ever operated on the South Park again.

Jull went on to build a total of eleven Excavators, but lack of interest in his plow forced him out of business in 1892. He returned to Canada, where he lived the remainder of his life in obscurity. The Leslie Rotary quickly became the darling of snow removal and remained the standard plow for many years. Despite the snow-plow trials, Alpine Pass remained out of service to through traffic. The next train over the line was Dad Martinis'—the ill-fated trip of 1895.

The Great Blockade of 1899

The South Park was, of course, not the only Colorado railroad to suffer from terrible snowfall. All the lines over the Rockies had to cope with the evils of winter operation. One of the hardest-hit lines was Colorado Midland's standard-gauge Continental Divide crossing at Hagerman Pass. Like Alpine Pass, Hagerman Pass crossed the Saguache Range in central Colorado west of Leadville. The high-line crossing at Hagerman Pass consisted of a series of tight horseshoe loops that scaled the side of the pass. It was one of the most visually impressive railroads, featuring many snowsheds and several long wooden trestles, including a great curving trestle on the west slope. A lower crossing of Hagerman Pass was completed in 1893 through a long bore known as the Ivanhoe-Busk Tunnel. This route was operated for a few years, but railroad management was unhappy with what they felt were exorbitant charges for use of the tunnel. The railroad resumed operations on their high line over the mountains in 1897. This choice proved disastrous when, a little more than a year later, following the easy winter of 1897–98, the railroad suffered one of the worst winters in its history.

Colorado Midland was an early supporter of the Leslie Rotary, acquiring the tenth plow built by the Cooke Works in December of 1887. This tool was invaluable in the railroad's battle with a seventy-seven-day blockade of its Hagerman Pass crossing.

January 24, 1899, saw a great storm blow in. It lasted for days and dumped vast quantities of snow in the mountains. Colorado Midland deployed armies of snow shovelers to keep its yards clear and sent its prized Rotary plow up the pass, with six powerful locomotives. On this first day of one of the worst snowstorms in Colorado history, the Rotary encountered deep drifts, nearly as high as the plow's great whirling fan. The tremendous snow fell unceasingly. By January 27, the situation had become desperate. Several crucial snowsheds collapsed under the weight of the still-falling snow, stranding trains on the east side of the pass. Meanwhile, the Rotary toiled to clear the west slope. It soon became stranded when a great avalanche destroyed the snowsheds protecting the high line's summit tunnel. The crew of an eastbound freight was forced to abandon their train and walk through the deep snow to safety. In his book *The Colorado Midland Railway*, Dan Abbott relates a series of fascinating narratives by the heroic men who fought the snow that fateful winter. Jack Hickman, the fireman on Colorado Midland helper engine No. 13, a recently overhauled Ten-Wheeler, operated by engineer Ike Kissel, describes his experience.

> *January 27, 1899 Ike & I were called to help Train No. 41 of that day to Thomasville. We started up the hill toward Busk, in a terrific blizzard. We knew the rotary was working somewhere ahead of us.*
>
> *When we arrived at Busk, we found the westbound passenger train had been halted there. The crew and the Busk operator gave us plenty of bad news. The rotary outfit was over on the west side of Hagerman Pass, cut off from us and Leadville by a huge slide beyond Hagerman tunnel. Just up the hill from Busk, snowsheds had collapsed and a stock train was snowed in. We couldn't back to Leadville, since the track behind us was full of snow. So there we sat!*

Jack Hickman did not know it then, but it would be nearly three months before the railroad was again clear of snow and opened to traffic!

SNOWBOUND!

Donner Pass, synonymous with vast quantities of snow, is one of the few places in American railroading where a passenger train has been snowbound in modern times. In December during a dry year, one might wander about Norden, California, and find only a trace of snowfall. But in the wet years, it is not unheard of for more than two hundred inches (508cm) of snow to be on the ground at one time.

On a cold January night in 1952, during one of the wet winters, the westbound *City of San Francisco*, Southern Pacific's streamlined passenger train, was making its way over Donner Pass. Storm after storm had blown in off the Pacific Ocean, dumping great quantities of snow in the Sierra. This line had once been covered by many miles of snowsheds, but in 1952 only a few crucial locations remained covered by sheds. At Norden, the covered operations center at the summit, the *City* was held by dispatchers while rotary plows cleared snowslides that had buried the tracks on the west side of the mountain. After some delay, the train was allowed to depart the cozy haven of the sheds and continue its westward journey on a route surveyed by Theodore Judah some

ninety years earlier—a tortuous route that hugged the open rock face of the mountain side. At Yuba Pass, less than twenty miles west of the Norden sheds, the train encountered a fresh snowslide.

No sheds protected the track. In near-blizzard conditions, snow quickly enveloped the train, trapping it at this remote location. The *City's* three modern Alco PA diesel-electric locomotives could not free the train and its many passengers from the icy clutches of the snow. A rotary plow pushed by a steam locomotive was dispatched from Norden to assist the stranded *City*, but every attempt to free the train proved futile. In short order, the train's situation went from inconvenient to desperate; winds were blowing snow in excess of forty miles per hour (64kph), and snow continued to fall. A relief train was sent up on the eastbound track with an army of workers equipped with shovels. But despite their valiant efforts to free the train, they were incapable of making significant progress; it was just snowing too hard. Soon the train's steam generator, which provided heat to the passenger car, had to be shut down, and food supplies began to run low. As the snow continued to fall, it became nearly impossible to reach the train by rail. A second rotary train had stalled trying to reach Yuba Pass. Worse, the engineer of a third rotary had been killed in a derailment when his plow encountered a snowslide. Brave men, alerted to the dire situation aboard the *City*, used snowshoes to hike overland from the nearby villages of Cisco and Nyack to bring needed supplies to the train's crew and passengers.

Finally, after three days of the worst winter weather imaginable, the storm ended; the sky became a clear, blue dome; and the stranded passengers were finally able to escape. A path was cleared alongside the snowbound train and down to U.S. Highway 40, which had also been closed in the storm. The passengers, grateful to be free from their frozen train, made their way to the road and were driven to a waiting relief train. Another three days passed before Southern Pacific work crews could finally free the *City of San Francisco* from the drifted snow.

LEFT: Rescuers wearing snowshoes hiked for miles to reach the snowbound train. There were no fatalities aboard the passenger train, although one man was killed on a snow plow trying to reach the stranded streamliner. OPPOSITE: In January 1952, Southern Pacific's *City of San Francisco* became snowbound on the west slope of the Sierra at Yuba Pass, California.

CHAPTER SIX

WRECKS AND ROBBERIES

OPPOSITE: *The most sensational sort of train wreck was the dreaded "head on." The fascination with train wrecks led enterprising promoters to stage public "cornfield meets." Tickets were sold, and locomotives—usually older surplus engines—were raced toward one another for the sole purpose of spectacle.*

TRAIN WRECKS

In the days before the advent of telephones, radio, air brakes, and modern automatic block signaling, train handling was a tricky and dangerous business. Railroaders relied upon their skill and experience to get trains over the road safely. Danger lay around every bend, and every run was an adventure. Trains were conducted by the rules, but according to an age-old railroader's saying, "There is a body behind every rule in the book." Even when rules were obeyed to the letter, there were still accidents and foul-ups.

One of the greatest fears of the traveling public in the early days of railroad travel was the dreaded head-on collision—sometimes called a "cornfield meet"—where two engineers, each one believing he had a clear track ahead, would charge their trains at each other at full speed. The result was often a fiery collision and sometimes great loss of life. This dreaded accident was not nearly as common as the rear-end collision, where a slowed or stopped train would be struck by a second train racing up from behind.

Although safety was an issue from the earliest days of railroading, oversights, overzealous operators, or unforeseen situations occasionally resulted in tragedy. Normally, trains did not

RIGHT: *Before the development of the Automatic Air Brake by George Westinghouse, brakemen would routinely ride on top of freight cars and turn down brakes by hand to slow a train down. The air brake reduced, but did not eliminate, the need for such dangerous activities.* **BELOW**: *Head-on collisions were one of the most feared type of railroad disaster. This one occurred on the Central Pacific at Tule, Nevada, on March 1, 1869, during the construction of the railroad.*

operate blindly. To prevent collisions, while allowing trains to make respectable time over the rails, there was a control system using timetables and train orders. Scheduled trains were operated under a class system, and preordained meeting points were listed in the timetable. It was understood that trains of inferior class were to get out of the way of superior trains. Unscheduled trains were issued train orders by a dispatcher who gave them operating authority on a specific section of track. The orders were delivered by telegraph to order stations and then given to the train crews by employees called operators. The telegraph operators were an integral part of the system, and they were known by a number of nicknames, including "brass pounders," which referred to the brass telegraph keys. Telegraph lines were strung alongside railroad tracks around the country. For more than a century telegraph lines and tracks were both synonymous with railroad transportation.

Trains that did not have orders were generally prohibited from moving. In some situations, however, they could travel at restricted speed, that is, a speed slow enough to stop in one half sight distance. Problems most often occurred in these uncertain situations.

For example, suppose the regular fast passenger train is delayed. When it fails to show up at its prescribed meeting point, the freight train waiting for it there decides to move to the next meeting point on "smoke orders," a term given to an engineer's creeping along without dispatcher's instruction, anxiously looking for an opposing train's telltale smoke on the horizon. Suddenly the freight encounters the fast passenger on a blind curve, and it's moving extra fast to make up lost time! The results are catastrophic.

Other problems were caused by mechanical failures. One common problem plaguing railroaders were "hotboxes," failures caused by excessive friction between the axle and journal. If it was caught in time, the hotbox would only result in a delay. If ignored, the axle could melt and result in a derailment or pileup.

Slowing and stopping trains on steep grades were always concerns. In the days before the advent of the Westinghouse Air Brake—which allowed the engineer to set brakes throughout the train from the locomotive—brakemen would have to set train brakes by hand. On freight trains, the brakemen would walk along the tops of the cars on narrow catwalks and turn down brake wheels. The engineer would sound "down brakes" or "up brakes" by a coded series of steam whistles. The brakemen were at constant risk of bodily harm. They were exposed in all kinds of weather. An inattentive brakeman who neglected to notice a tunnel, snowshed, or other overhead obstacle might be knocked off the moving train.

While the advent of the air brake improved train handling, brakemen would often still have to walk the cars to operate manual brakes in mountainous territory, where air brakes alone did not provide sufficient braking, and also when cold weather or other problems snarled the air lines. The air brakes relied upon an airline to maintain pressure throughout the train. They were held apart by constant air pressure provided by an air pump on the locomotive. To set the brakes, the engineer would make a "reduction" to the air line, reducing the pressure and allowing the brake shoes to act on the wheels. If the engineer released all of the air at once, a procedure called "dumping the air" or "putting the train in emergency," the trains brakes would act suddenly, an action that could itself cause a derailment.

The problems railroaders encountered were greatly magnified on steep mountain grades, and the pay scale for mountain work reflected this. But it was winter operations in the mountains that had a well-deserved nightmarish reputation. One common problem with air brakes was ice in the airline. This "bottled the air," preventing the engineer from making a brake application. If the engineer did not have full control of his brakes on a steep grade, he might be unable to retain control of the train. This was the greatly feared runaway—a disaster that sent many railroaders to their deaths. In some cases runaway freight trains would attain tremendous speed before rounding a tight curve and spilling into a deep ravine.

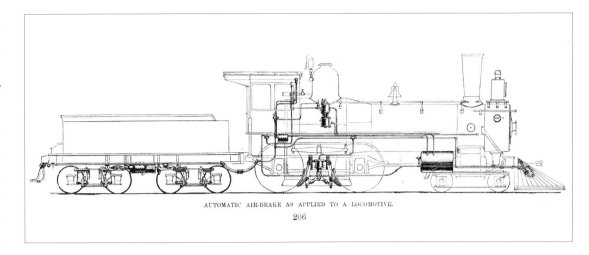

AUTOMATIC AIR-BRAKE AS APPLIED TO A LOCOMOTIVE.
206

Broken rails, washouts caused by flash floods, locomotive boiler explosions, overweight trains on flimsy wooden trestles, botched orders sent by confused dispatchers, and overeager crews taking needless chances all caused their fair share of railroad wrecks. The topic of wrecks was never a popular one among railroaders because everyone running trains had to work in the face of perilous dangers, and all knew fellow railroaders who had gone on a run and never come back. Western railroading in particular has a legacy of railroad disasters. Some of the stories are legends; others are personal accounts by those who witnessed an event, or its grisly aftermath. Newspapers loved good stories, even when the events were of minor importance, and there was no better headline than the good, old-fashioned "Train Wreck"—even when it was no more than a derailed boxcar in a yard. Every so often the real thing occurred, and some of the most dramatic tales of the railroad are those of its misadventures.

Head On!

On the eastern shore of San Francisco Bay, on the morning of November 15, 1869, a six-car, Stockton-bound Western Pacific passenger train was running late and trying to make up time. Orders had been given to a switch tender to make a meet between this train and another running from Hayward to Alameda. But the switch tender was incompetent and misread his orders. The racing Stockton train was sent head on into the path of the other. Seeing impending doom, the engineer of the Alameda train jumped from his seat, and his life was spared. Moments later the trains collided, creating a shower of splinters

ABOVE: *The development of the Westinghouse Air Brake greatly improved railroad safety. Although the advantages of the air brake were obvious, it was still nearly thirty years before the railroad industry adopted it universally.*

and wreckage. The wooden cars crumpled and disintegrated. Bodies were thrown about like rag dolls. When the dust had settled, more than fifteen were dead, including both the engineer and fireman of the Stockton-bound train and the unlucky fireman of the Alameda train. At the time it was the worst train wreck in the West and the *San Francisco Chronicle* covered it in spectacular terms: "The crash was terrific. . . . The carnage was horrible! Twelve corpses were counted on the spot. . . ."

Runaway Trains

Few lines in the West have a greater mystique than the Colorado Midland. Its legacy was one of exceptional terrain and primeval mountain operations. Its accidents are Western legends. In his book *Colorado Midland Railway: Daylight Through the Divide*, author Dan Abbott chronicles this fascinating railroad's history and woeful misadventures.

The Colorado Midland's formidable 4-percent grades—a drop of 211 feet per mile (40m per kilometer)—were among the steepest ever employed on a standard-gauge mainline. The railroad was keenly aware of the problems of such steep grades and enforced strict train-handling procedures to ensure safe

BELOW: *Wrecks would frequently incur public outrage; concerns about railroad safety inspired a cartoonist to suggest a safer way of railroad travel.*

running. Nonetheless, these rules were sometimes ignored, with deadly results.

On the evening of July 15, 1891, an eastbound thirteen-car Colorado Midland freight, led by locomotive No. 4, rolled into Cascade Cañon, Colorado. Engineer Maurice Moore, a veteran mountain railroader, was at the throttle and James P. Wilson was his fireman. No. 4 was a 2-8-0 Consolidation built by the Schenectady Locomotive Works of Schenectady, New York, in 1887. In most respects it was typical of heavy freight locomotives of the time. While waiting at Cascade Cañon for two westbound trains to pass, crews inspected the train and ran an air test to check the Westinghouse Brakes—a routine procedure mandated by the rules. The train had just descended a long section of 3-percent grade and was now resting on a relatively level spot. Ahead of the train lay one of the steepest sections of line—the dreaded 4-percent, and every precaution was encouraged before attempting its descent.

The danger of a runaway was of sufficient concern to the railroad that they had installed a manned runaway track partway down the grade called the "safety switch." This was a sidetrack that diverged from the mainline on a steep ascent and served no other purpose than to enable a careening train to save itself from doom. A switchman was stationed there at all hours. The switch was kept lined for the runaway track, and only on the signal from a descending train—three whistles: one long, one short, and another long—would the line be switched to the main. Eight hundred feet (244m) from the switch, a marker was placed as a cue for the engineer to blow his whistle.

Engineer Moore held the runaway track in contempt. On several occasions he boasted he would rather risk the mainline than take the safety switch, probably a common attitude among the sure-footed men in those wild days. Safety measures were merely to satisfy the weak-willed hearts of managers, stockholders, and other lesser men. Men of courage didn't need such devices; they could rely solely on clear-headedness and skill.

The brakemen tied down three hand brakes each, and at nearly 1:00 a.m., the train eased down the grade. Moore made a reduction to the air line, to hold the train to 12½ miles an hour (20kph), the maximum allowable speed on the six miles (10km) of descending 4-percent grade. However, the train's speed continued to increase and was soon far greater than the maximum. Alarmed, the brakemen scrambled to tighten down the hand

brakes. Their efforts were in vain, and soon the train was racing at more than twenty miles an hour (32kph). The one thing that could save them was the safety switch. And, surely, everyone on the train anticipated a ride up the "safety." Everyone except Moore, who blew one long, one short, and one long at the eight hundred foot (244m) mark. The switchman lined the track for the main. As the train raced toward destiny, Moore made a last effort to slow his train by reversing the locomotive. Moments before the train reached the safety switch, the switchman ran to reverse it, but it was too late. There wasn't time, and the east-bound train flew by.

The brakemen jumped from their posts and the conductor uncoupled his caboose. The conductor quickly brought the separated caboose to a stop and met the two shaken brakemen. The three men proceeded cautiously, fearing the worst.

Two miles (3km) beyond the safety switch was a sharp curve and a tunnel. Moore and No. 4 never made it to the tunnel; the train left the track just before its west portal. The engine crashed into a wall of solid granite and the train piled up behind. When the conductor reached the scene he found Mr. Moore, sitting woefully by the tunnel portal. He was badly burned and very confused. Before he died, he asked what had gone wrong. He thought his train was under control until moments before the crash. Fireman Wilson however did not survive the impact, and his body, buried under tons of coal, took twenty hours to dig out. In the end the railroad attributed the wreck to Moore's mis-handling. Engine No. 4 was rebuilt and served the railroad for another twenty-five years.

Operations on the rugged Colorado Midland remained per-ilous throughout its short life. Another of its steep grades, the

ABOVE: *Wrecks were not a pop-ular topic among railroaders; their lives and livelihoods were at stake. Fatalities from train wrecks were most often railroad employees. This freight train piled up on the Western Pacific.*

above Turquoise Lake. Locomotive No. 6 plunged more than two hundred feet (61m) down the side of the mountain, bringing most of the train with it.

Engineer Forrest rode his engine down. The crash broke his leg and killed the fireman, Marshall Rich. The impact of the derailment crushed the caboose against the rear two cars at track level in a rock cut, killing the rear brakeman and the conductor. The head brakeman was seriously injured, but not killed. And an unfortunate passenger—a hobo hitching a ride in one of the freight cars—was also injured.

Narrow-gauge Rio Grande Southern had its fair share of mishaps and crashes on its tortuous mountain crossings. Josie Crum lists tale after tale of the trials and tribulations of mountain railroading. Not all runaway trains proved fatal, and some men lived to tell their tales in person. Crum relates a story told by Barney and Temple Cornelius.

A freight train was on its way from Rico to Durango in January, 1904 with Barney Cornelius as the engineer.

They had been ordered to pick up some cars of coal at Ute Junction which, added to what they already had, made a very heavy train. As it was late at night and terribly cold, the brakes on the coal cars were icy and stiff.

This was in the days of straight air, link and pin couplers and hand brakes. After the train started down the mainline, it began to gain speed and Cornelius could not make enough air to set the brakes. He called for hand brakes but they were not sufficient, especially as those on the coal cars were working poorly. According to the engineer, the train just flew, but by some good fortune, stayed on the tracks around the Mule Shoe curve. They succeeded in getting stopped at Pine Ridge where the grade leveled off.

What to do then was the problem—to take a chance on another runaway or set the train out on a siding. After some deliberation they decided to take the chance. Soon the train started running away again, rolling past Porter, through Wild Cat Canon, over the high trestle at Lightner Creek and onto the grade leading into the Durango yards. The joke of it was that when they stopped at the top of the hill and threw the switch onto the mainline they couldn't get started again. As it was night no switch engine was on duty and they had to cut the train in two and take it into the yard in sections.

ABOVE: *Colorado Midland's Hagerman Pass crossing was one of the most amazing railroads ever constructed. The railroad made four loops while ascending the east slope. The tracks on the left go toward the Hagerman Tunnel, while those on the right go toward Leadville.*

OPPOSITE: *Train wreck on the Santa Fe. Before the development of roller bearings, hotboxes— caused by excessive axle friction— would frequently result in massive pileups. Broken rails and rock slides are another frequent cause of railroad accidents.*

Continental Divide crossing at Hagerman Pass west of Leadville, was the source of considerable consternation, particularly in the winter. Hagerman was one of the highest crossings of the divide and featured many miles of treacherous cliffside running and steep 3-percent grades.

On a very cold day in January 1910, Locomotive Engineer Harry Forrest took the throttle of a heavily loaded, ten-car, eastbound freight at Cardiff, Colorado. He had more than a sixty-mile (97km) climb to the top of Hagerman Pass, then a sharp drop down the other side. His locomotive was No. 6, a Schenectady-built 2-8-0 Consolidation, and the sister engine of No. 4, which had crashed coming down Cascade Cañon. The ride up the pass was routine. The train climbed through the long Ivanhoe-Busk tunnel at the divide without incident, but shortly after leaving the east portal, on the descent of the east slope, the train ran into trouble. As the train began to gain speed heading down the grade, Harry Forrest applied the air brakes—without result. Ice in the line had bottled the air. As the train began to race headlong out of control, he signaled for the brakemen to set the hand brakes. They scrambled frantically along the tops of the cars, tying down the hand brakes. Their efforts were to no avail. The train continued inexorably to gain momentum on the steep grade. The brakemen and conductor scrambled back to the caboose, reaching it just as the train hit a very sharp curve high

The Burlington & Missouri River line operated the Black Hills & Fort Pierre Railroad in southwestern South Dakota for a short time around the turn of the century. In 1902 Jim Bullard was working as a young brakeman on the line. Mildred Fielder relates his experiences on that narrow-gauge line in her book, *Railroads of the Black Hills*.

This narrow gauge railroading was apart from any other kind. It was hard, cruel, dangerous. Many died, were crippled for life or just could not take it and walked off the job. Bucking snow was one of the cold chilly jobs that we went through in the hills each winter. We would try one engine with no luck, then get another. Sometimes we would take three of those little narrow gauge hogs tied together, back off and take a run at the drift and then not break through.

Runaways were the thing the narrow gauge men dreaded. Once they got a good start they were gone and you went with them. The only way to prevent them was club 'em tight with the good old brakie's friend, the brake club, and when you heard that long sharp blast from the hogger you knew it was time to tie 'em down just a little harder or you were gone.

Jim Bullard spoke from experience. He had the misfortune to ride a careening train down a grade and, like Barney Cornelius, lived to tell about it:

The biggest thrill I ever had in my 49 years and three months on the shining steel was on the morning of July 12, 1902, going down the mountain from Woodville on the old Black Hills & Fort Pierre narrow gauge railroad. I was the only brakeman . . . big, good natured John Cooksey was the engineer, Hy Wamsley was the fireman, and the conductor was a long, tall freckled-faced fellow from Box Butte County, Tom Briggs. . . . After tipping the mountain I commenced setting hand brakes, but could not get much action out of those brakes on the flat cars. We did not have very many cars with air. When big John Cooksey the engineer commenced whistling for brakes I knew we were really running away.

When that little mountain hog, the 488, went around the curve she went down the dump, cars piled up behind her and yours truly went up in the air, came down and landed right between two big boulders where there was a nice bed of soft dirt

and sand that been whipped in there by the wind. Some landing! Cooksey and Hy Wamsley, the fireman, went clear of the engine as she turned over, and they both landed in the top of a tree without a bruise. We had a paymaster for the Homestake Company in the caboose and an old lady passenger with five dozen eggs going to Nemo to visit her son. The paymaster had a Winchester and $5,000 in silver and gold to pay off employees around Nemo and other stations along the line. They had a late pay day. It took five long days and night[s] to get that 488 back on the rails.

The little mountain climbers that wound their way up and down through the Black Hills are long since scrapped, but those of us who worked with them will never forget them.

Soon after that adventure, Jim Bullard gave up mountainous, narrow-gauge railroading for the safer, standard-gauge, flatland variety. He went to work for the Rock Island lines.

Runaway on Tehachapi

Heavy freight trains were more prone to running away than passenger trains were. But usually the only people killed on a runaway freight were railroad employees and the occasional freeloader. Passenger-train runaways, though far rarer, had much higher death tolls. Such accidents were horrifying and attracted considerably more attention than the freight disasters. By the late 1880s, passenger runaways had largely been brought to a halt. And one of the last great passenger-train runaways happened in the early days on the Southern Pacific.

The line over the picturesque Tehachapi Mountains in California had been completed in May of 1876. This route wound upward through rolling hills and past the villages of Caliente, Bealville, and Woodford before crossing over itself at the famous Tehachapi Loop, and then continued to climb to the summit at the town of Tehachapi. The ruling grade was a challenging 2.2 percent. Most trains, freight and passenger alike, required additional locomotives, known as "helpers" to get up to the top of the grade. Even with extra locomotives, progress was very slow because of the many tight curves and tunnels on the line.

On the evening of January 19, 1883, Southern Pacific No. 19, the *Atlantic Express*, a seven-car passenger train consisting of a

mail car, an express car, a baggage, two sleepers, a coach, and a smoker, climbed up through the Tehachapis. The smoker was a car reserved for male passengers—it gave them a place to smoke and chew tobacco without offending female passengers.

At Caliente near the base of the grade, No. 19 paused to pick up its helper, which was "cut in" behind the leading locomotive. The train continued from there to the summit at Tehachapi without any problems. It arrived around 2:00 a.m., and both locomotives were removed from the train to allow the helper to return down the mountain, leaving the cars uncoupled on the grade. All of No. 19's operating crew was away from the train. The head brakeman was assisting with turning the helper, the conductor was speaking with the telegraph operator at the depot, and the rear brakeman was attending to a young woman passenger whose pretty looks had distracted him. A fierce wind was blowing and the train's brake failed to hold the cars on the grade. Before anyone knew it, the seven cars, passengers soundly

sleeping aboard, began to roll away from the depot and back down the grade they had just climbed.

Before long, the engineless *Atlantic Express* was racing downgrade at great speed. As it squealed around the tight curves along Tehachapi Creek, the coal stoves toppled over and ignited the wooden cars. Some say the train was moving at more than seventy miles per hour (113kph) before it broke apart. The now-flaming sleepers, mail, express, and baggage cars plunged off the tracks, down a ravine, and into Tehachapi Creek. As they hit, the burning cars splintered and disintegrated, dumping some of their sleeping victims on the ground. Meanwhile, the coach and smoker continued unchecked down the grade. The passengers aboard the coach awoke and were able to secure the hand brakes, eventually bringing the wayward cars to a halt near Tunnel No. 11 just above Marcel, California. Some accounts indicate that the same brakeman who had been attending the young woman at Tehachapi noticed the train rolling away and leaped aboard, and

ABOVE: *Freight train derailments are far more common than passenger train wrecks. This derailment occurred in 1936 on the Burlington at Aurora, Illinois.*

that it was he who tied down the brakes in the smoker. Reports vary, but between fifteen and seventeen people died in the disaster. Among the casualties was Mrs. John Downey, the wife of the former governor of California; a former Wisconsin congressman was also killed.

One of train's passengers, Mr. Porter Ashe, gave his account of the wreck's aftermath in the San Francisco *Call*, related by Wesley S. Griswold in his book *Train Wreck!*

Our maid was buried in the debris, my wife and I falling on top of her. The car immediately took fire, and we were forced to take the timber and burning boards off the maid piece by piece. The car became enveloped in smoke. By breaking the windows at the top of the car, I succeeded in rescuing my wife and maid and pushed them through the window.

We were climbing off the car, nearly suffocated by the smoke, when I heard a man calling for help and beseeching us not to leave him. I reached down through a broken window and succeeded in getting hold of Governor Downey's hand and pulling him out, nearly strangled.

While helping her maid to the ground, my wife stepped on the window and fell through into the car again. The car by this

Wreck on the Denver & Rio Grande

time was burning rapidly. It is impossible to tell how I got her out. I jumped with her to the ground and immediately ran down the hill to avoid the flames.

Author Griswold compares this story with another, less vivid account and indicates that, in the heat of the moment, Ashe may have exaggerated his own heroics.

After the tragedy, the railroad issued a statment that suggested that saboteurs had tampered with the train in a botched robbery attempt. Despite these accusations, the train's crew was later arrested for negligence.

On the rainy Sunday evening of August 7, 1904, train No. 11, led by locomotive 1009, was running toward Pueblo from Denver, Colorado, with a heavy load of passengers. Some were weekend travelers who had visited Denver and Colorado Springs for a pleasant diversion. Others were long-distance passengers who would connect at Pueblo with an eastbound train on the Missouri Pacific. Lively spirits prevailed aboard the train as it wound up and over the Palmer Divide, making its way along the Front Range toward destiny. Light rain in the lowlands was not of much concern, but heavy rain at higher elevations was cause for worry. At Colorado Springs, the engineer was warned about heavy rain farther south and advised to take it easy. A normally dry wash could, in a moment of bad weather, become a raging torrent.

The heavy crowds and rain had delayed the train, and by the time it left Colorado Springs it had fallen a couple of hours behind schedule. It was nearly dark as it cautiously approached the tiny village of Eden, Colorado, more than one hundred miles (161km) south of Denver and only a few miles from Pueblo. Harry Hinman, the engineer, held the throttle at a steady fifteen to twenty miles per hour (24–32kph) as they crossed a spindly bridge over Hogan's Gulch. Midway across the short but high trestle, the train lurched. The rain had weakened the structure and the train's weight brought it down. In a desperate attempt, Hinman opened the throttle hoping to pull the train off the damaged bridge, but it was too late. The timbers snapped and the engine fell backward into the raging creek. The engine's fireman, David C. Mayfield, jumped away from the train as it fell. In a moment that seemed an eternity he watched as car after car loaded with passengers plunged after the engine. Only the last couple of cars were spared from tragedy, thanks to Mr. Westinghouse and his automatic air brake. Nearly one hundred people died in the wreck, including Engineer Hinman. It was one of the worst train wrecks in the West. Yet, as in other wrecks, the locomotive survived! It was dredged from the muddy gulch and rebuilt, and it operated for another thirty years.

OPPOSITE: *A derailed Western Pacific locomotive deep in the Feather River Canyon at milepost 277. The rocky nature of the Feather River Canyon in the California Sierra makes it prone to rock slides, which have derailed many trains over the years.*

HANDS UP!

Shortly after sundown on a summer's night in central Missouri, five men lie in the shadows trackside. The whistle of the westbound express can be heard in the distance. A pile of railroad ties and other heavy debris has been stacked between the rails. As the train comes around a shallow curve, the engineer spots the manmade obstruction and brings his train to a stop. Before the fireman has time to jump to the ground, two men brandishing revolvers enter the cab of the locomotive. Two others board the passenger cars and introduce themselves to the passengers. The fifth stays on the ground to make sure nothing goes wrong.

In just a few minutes the passengers, relieved of their gold, jewelry, and other valuables, nod nervously as the infamous train robber bids them adieu. A quick inspection of the express cars proves rewarding: they contain more than twelve thousand dollars of Uncle Sam's gold. The train robbers help themselves to this newfound wealth. Soon they are all off the train and galloping into the night.

The first conspicuous highway robberies in the West occurred in the 1850s, when horse-drawn stages loaded with gold from the Sierra were looted at gunpoint on winding mountain roads in California. The lure of easy money, which had attracted so many prospectors to California in 1849, also attracted those who were too lazy to dig for the gold.

One such stage robber was the notorious Black Bart, who wore a feed sack over his head and a distinctive white duster. In his illustrious robbing career he single-handedly knocked off some twenty-seven stagecoaches in the Sierra foothills of California. He robbed most of them at gunpoint and usually targeted stages carrying the United States Mail. Eventually he was apprehended, tried, and sentenced to six years in San Quentin prison.

Stage robbers kept busy. In the fourteen years between 1870 and 1884, some 313 Wells Fargo stages were robbed. This was a dangerous business, particularly for the perpetrators. The bandits had a high mortality rate. Law enforcement agents killed eleven of those targeting Wells Fargo in the act of robbing or shortly thereafter. Another seven were caught, tried, and hanged.

While it was a popular activity, stage robbing was not that lucrative. One notable stage bandit, Sam Bass, after holding up a stage in the vicinity of Deadwood, South Dakota, and netting some four hundred dollars, was quoted as saying, "Well, this is the best haul I have made out of a stage, and I have tapped nine of 'em so far. There's mighty poor pay in stages." Mr. Bass quickly moved on to bigger booty: banks and trains.

The first reported train robbery in the United States happened at Marshfield, Indiana, along the Jeffersonville Railroad, a year before the Promontory Golden Spike ceremony. The Reno gang robbed an express car at gunpoint and made off into the night.

The most famous of all train robbers, a man who catapulted the crime into American mythology, was Jesse James. James worked in tandem with his brother Frank, and their cousins the Younger brothers—formidable train robbers in their own right. The legend of Jesse James is that of a modern-day Robin Hood. He was feared for his deeds, but James inspired awe in many who viewed the railroad and its riders as evil and greedy. He plied his trade at a time of growing antirailroad sentiment and post–Civil War hostility toward anything and anyone from the North.

James was born on September 5, 1847, in Clay County, Missouri. At a young age he became an ardent supporter of the Confederacy in the War Between the States. He was part of W. C. Quantrill's guerrilla group, and from this experience he undoubtedly learned much of what he needed for his later robbing profession. James was a fugitive from justice for most of his adult life.

In 1866 James and his gang held up the bank at Liberty, Missouri, becoming responsible for the first bank robbery in the West. But they did not begin robbing trains until July 31, 1873.

That evening James and his gang derailed and robbed an express train east of Council Bluffs, Iowa. A locomotive and seven cars were sent tumbling off the iron rails. In the wreck the engineer was scalded to death from boiler steam, and the fireman was seriously injured. All of the passengers aboard the train were robbed at gunpoint, and James and company made off into the Iowa night on horseback with nearly three thousand dollars. But they had botched the job! They had derailed the wrong train. The express they had intended to rob was supposedly carrying more than $100,000 in gold. James learned from this mistake. In the future he would have to pay closer attention to railroad schedules!

Another heist proved far more rewarding for James. He and four members of his gang came into the tiny frontier hamlet of Muncie, Kansas, a little west of Kansas City. James was not one to waste time in idleness, so he and his bandits held up the general store. The booty was pocket change, but the robbery fended off the boredom of waiting for a train. To stop the express James merely piled ties on the tracks. Perhaps he felt that derailing trains had proved too messy. As the express eased to a stop before the obstruction, the bandits boarded the train brandishing their six-shooters. The train's conductor was nearly shot dead when he was spotted running down the tracks. Even under the duress of the robbery, the faithful conductor was true to his duty. Compelled to return to the train, he hastily explained to his new pistol-equipped bosses that he needed to protect the train's rear. A fast freight was following, and if he failed to post a flag, it would run up from behind and collide with this train. The bandits acquiesced, and the conductor went on to fulfill his obligations. In the meantime, the safe in the express car was breached, and the James gang rode off with more than fifty thousand dollars in gold and jewelry. Before departing, James is reported to have said sardonically to the train's terrified passengers, "Give our love to the folks in Kansas City."

James went on robbing trains and banks for another seven years. Occasionally he would "retire" for a period of time, to enjoy the fruits of his labor. He traveled widely across the South and West. His last train robbery occurred on July 15, 1881. He had not robbed any trains for a while and was getting a little rusty. Four members of his gang boarded a six-car Rock Island train, No. 2, at Cameron, Missouri. When the train pulled into the next station to the east, another four bandits boarded the train. As the train got under way, James went into action. All eight men drew their weapons and shouted at passengers to throw up their hands. Two bandits started toward the tender, where they intended to commandeer the train.

The train's conductor was not taken with the idea of following instructions issued at gunpoint from nonrailroad personnel. He ran from his assailants toward the rear of the train. Without hesitation the bandits shot and killed him as he reached the rear platform. His body fell from the train as it made its eastward progress across the plains. Having killed one man, the bandits felt no qualm about killing others, and when a sleeping-car passenger gave them trouble they shot him, too.

OPPOSITE: *Train robbers were often familiar with railroad schedules, yet it was not unusual for bandits to make a mistake and rob the wrong train. The difference was often costly.*

RIGHT: *Jesse James spent most of his adult life as a fugitive from the law; he is one of the West's most infamous desperadoes.*

FAR RIGHT: *While Jesse James was shot and killed, his brother Frank lived to a ripe old age. Frank died in 1915, outliving his more famous brother by thirty-three years.*

All of a sudden the train screeched to a halt—the brakemen had dumped the air. The bandits on the tender dropped down into the cab of the engine and demanded the engineer move the train. They were displeased when he spat back at them that the air had set the brakes and he could not move the train. Angry, one bandit took aim at the railroader, intending to route him the same way as his conductor, but he missed. The engineer doused the light in the cab, jumped through the window out onto the engine, and hid. The bandits took charge of the train, waited for the air to bleed off, and then proceeded forward to the predesignated place where they were to rob the train. Inside the express car, James and his men forced open the safe and helped themselves to the paltry six hundred dollars in cash and non-negotiable paper there. Disgusted, James rode off into the darkness, leaving the bodies of his victims behind.

This botched robbery proved to be James's undoing. When word circulated about the atrocities committed, Rock Island offered a five-thousand-dollar reward for information leading to apprehension of the James Gang. The governor of Missouri upped the ante, offering five thousand dollars for each member of the gang, and an additional five thousand dollars for its outlaw leader. In April 1882, this reward finally caught up with the renowned outlaw hero. A former fellow gunman, Bob Ford, shot Jesse James in the head. Soon afterward Frank James was captured and sent to prison. While the West's most famous bandit was out of business for good, others took his place, and the glamorous act of train robbing continued.

The peak of Western train robbing was in the 1880s. Yet there were still some 260 armed railroad robberies in the 1890s. It was a risky business, and two thirds of all those involved were either killed on the job or captured and executed after the fact. By 1900 this crime had been virtually eliminated, and those who perpetrated it had been imprisoned or hanged.

Romantic accounts of Western train robberies in the 1870s and 1880s made a lasting impression. Hollywood and popular magazines perpetuated the mythology of the outlaw hero, glorifying the crime and instilling sentimental notions into the American imagination.

The last-known Western train robbery was inspired by the glorified train-robber myths of the earlier era. In 1923, many years after the tradition of train robbing had succumbed to more civilized ways of life, the three DeAutremont brothers, of southern Oregon, decided to improve their impoverished circumstances by following the example of the glorious train-robber gangs. Perhaps they were intrigued with the adventures of Jesse James and the Youngers. Or maybe the Doolins, the Daltons, or the legendary Sam Bass of Texas caught their imagination. Certainly, the DeAutremont brothers had studied the methods of train robbery; their attempt closely followed historical precedent. The legends of train robbing tended to highlight the adventure and reward of the crime, but rarely mentioned mortality statistics for the perpetrators.

They picked a suitable location for their crime: Southern Pacific's steep, tortuous crossing of the Siskiyou Mountains south of Ashland, Oregon. This mountain grade features several tunnels and trestles, and fits the profile of railroads depicted in American literature. More important, it was close by. At the summit of the grade was a long tunnel situated amidst tall firs and spruce. The secluded west portal of the tunnel was sufficiently isolated for a classic Western robbery. Here, on the morning of October 11, 1923, Ray DeAutremont lay in wait, preparing for his first train robbery and no doubt dreaming of how to spend his newly acquired riches. Meanwhile, his brothers waited on the other side of the tunnel for upbound train No. 13, a section of the *San Francisco Express* carrying the United States Mail and coach passengers. A second train would follow close behind with Pullman sleepers, but this was not their concern; they were after lucrative booty hidden with the mail.

At 11:30 a.m. engineer Sid Bates opened the throttle of engine 3626, a big 2-10-2–type designed for hauling trains in the mountains, and departed rural Ashland at the bottom of the grade. Slowly and surely he plodded up the 3-percent grade toward Siskiyou Summit. He wound through the horseshoe curves at Steinmen, then rolled around the loops below Wall Creek, and finally made his way up and over the tall, spindly Wall Creek trestle. The DeAutremonts followed the train's slow progress, listening to the syncopated rhythms of the big engine as it worked its way up the mountain. In their anticipation, they may have wondered why Southern Pacific had not found a less circuitous crossing of the Siskiyous, and cursed the train for not

making swifter progress. Finally, after a half hour of climbing, the train crawled up to the summit. There Hugh and Roy DeAutremont leapt aboard, weapons in hand. In no time the train dove into the Summit Tunnel, and in the darkness, the bandits made their way to the cab. Under threats of violence, they persuaded Engineer Bates to stop his train at the west portal of the tunnel. Against his better judgment, he complied with their demands. Ray DeAutremont was waiting for them with dynamite. Using their crude explosives, the three novice train robbers attempted to blow the door off the baggage-mail car. The result was disastrous for all involved. The ensuing explosion destroyed the car and its contents and killed its attendant, Elvyn Dougherty. The brothers, having botched the robbery, but presumably still hoping to recover some booty, insisted that the remains of the mail car be uncoupled and towed ahead. The train crew was unable to meet their demands because of the extensive damage from the explosion. Exasperated by their mistakes (train robbing seemed so easy in the magazines!), the DeAutremonts brutally shot and killed three members of the train crew, including Engineer Bates.

Having murdered four men, and without a cent to show for it, the three brothers made off into the hills. They remained at large for three years, but were eventually caught, tried, and sentenced to life in prison—thus closing the last chapter in Western train robbery.

ABOVE: *The mythology of the train robbery has fed the legend of the lawlessness of the American West. By 1900, train robberies were rare. This one was staged for a photographer in 1907, undoubtedly with the cooperation of the railroad!*

Bibliography

Abbott, Dan. *Colorado Midland Railway: Daylight Through the Divide.* Denver, Colorado, 1989.

Athearn, Robert G. *Rebel of the Rockies: The Denver & Rio Grande Western Railroad.* New Haven, Connecticut, 1962.

Beebe, Lucius. *The Central Pacific and the Southern Pacific Railroads.* Berkeley, California, 1963.

_____. *Mr. Pullman's Elegant Palace Car.* New York, New York, 1961.

_____. *The Overland Limited.* Berkeley, California, 1963.

Beebe, Lucius, and Charles Clegg. *Hear the Train Blow.* New York, New York, 1952.

_____. *Narrow Gauge in the Rockies.* Berkeley, California, 1958.

Best, Gerald M. *Snowplow: Clearing Mountain Rails.* Berkeley, California, 1966.

Brown, Dee. *Hear That Lonesome Whistle Blow.* New York, New York, 1977.

Bryant, Keith L. *History of the Atchison, Topeka & Santa Fe Railway.* New York, New York, 1974.

Ira G. *Then Came the Railroads.* Norman, Oklahoma, 1958.

Crum, Josie Moore. *The Rio Grande Southern Railroad.* Durango, Colorado, 1961.

Deverell, William. *Railroad Crossing: The Californian and the Railroad, 1850–1910.* Berkeley, California, 1994.

Dubin, Arthur D. *Some Classic Trains.* Milwaukee, Wisconsin, 1964.

Dunscomb, Guy L. *A Century of Southern Pacific Steam Locomotives.* Modesto, California, 1963.

Fielder, Mildred. *Railroads of the Black Hills.* Seattle, Washington, 1964.

Griswold, Wesley S. *Train Wreck!* Brattleboro, Vermont, 1969.

_____. *A Work of Giants: Building the First Transcontinental Railroad.* New York, New York, 1962.

Hauck, Cornelius W.; Gordon Chappell; and Robert W. Richardson. *The South Park Line: A Concise History.* Golden, Colorado, 1976.

Hedges, J.B. *Henry Villard and the Railways of the Northwest.* New Haven, Connecticut, 1930.

Hinckley, Helen. *Rails from the West: A Biography of Theodore D. Judah.* San Marino, California, 1969.

Holbrook, Stewart H. *The Age of the Moguls.* Garden City, New York, 1954.

Lewis, Oscar. *The Big Four.* New York, New York, 1938.

McCarty, Lea F. *The Gunfighters.* Berkeley, California, 1959.

McCoy, Dell, and Russ Collman. *"The Rio Grande Pictorial": One Hundred Years of Railroading Through the Rockies.* Denver, Colorado, 1971.

Malone, Michael P. *James J. Hill: Empire Builder of the Northwest.* Norman, Oklahoma, 1996.

Marshal, James. *Santa Fe: The Railroad That Built an Empire.* New York, New York, 1945.

Morse, Frank P. *Cavalcade of the Rails.* New York, New York, 1940.

O'Connor, Richard. *Iron Wheels and Broken Men.* New York, New York, 1973.

Riegel, Robert Edgar. *The Story of the Western Railroads.* Lincoln, Nebraska, 1926.

Russell, Don. *Trails of the Iron Horse.* Garden City, New York, 1975.

Signor, John R. *Rail in the Shadow of Mt. Shasta.* San Diego, California, 1982.

_____. *Tehachapi.* San Marino, California, 1983.

Shearer, Fredrick E. *The Pacific Tourist.* New York, New York, 1970.

Sinclair, Angus. *Development of the Locomotive Engine.* New York, New York, 1907.

Waters, L.L. *Steel Trails to Santa Fe.* Lawrence, Kansas, 1950.

Williams, John Hoyt. *A Great and Shining Road.* New York, New York, 1988.

Wilson, Neill C., and Frank J. Taylor. *Southern Pacific: The Roaring Story of a Fighting Railroad.* New York, New York, 1952.

Winther, Oscar Osburn. *The Transportation Frontier: Trans-Mississippi West, 1865–1890.* New York, New York, 1964.

PERIODICALS

Locomotive & Railway Preservation. Waukesha, Wisconsin.

Pacific Rail News. Waukesha, Wisconsin.

Trains. Waukesha, Wisconsin.

Photo Credits